WARSAW

ANDRZEJ ROTTERMUND

WARSAW

PHOTOGRAPHS:

MIROSŁAW AND MACIEJ CIUNOWICZ

ARKADY

The statue of the Mermaid standing on the Old Town Market Square, by Konstanty Hegel

Panorama of Warsaw; view of the Royal Castle and the Old Town seen from the Praga district

←

ontents

From the Author ———————————— 9

Spatial Plan ———————————— 13

The Old and New Towns ———————————— 51

The Royal Castle ———————————— 95

The city centre ———————————— 145

Royal Residences
at Łazienki and Wilanów ———————————— 237

Beyond the city centre ———————————— 259

Praga ———————————— 275

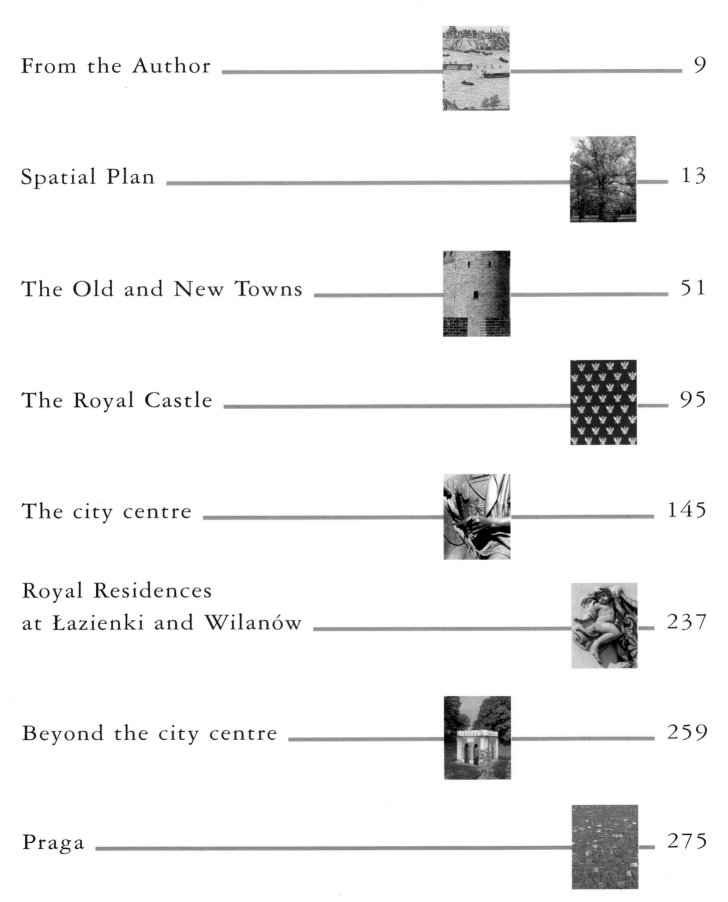

The decision concerning the reconstruction of the Royal Castle in Warsaw, made in January 1971, led to producing up to twenty publications associated with the history of the Castle and its immediate surroundings. An outstanding example was the album Stare Miasto i Zamek Królewski (The Old Town and the Royal Castle), issued by the Arkady publishing house. Three outlines by Professors Piotr Biegański, Stanisław Lorentz and Jan Zachwatowicz – eminent scholars dealing with the history of Warsaw and foremost contributors to the reconstruction of the Royal Castle – presented the Castle in a wider framework as an "architectural organism", whose past was always connected with the city and its history.

The proposed album relates to that publication, aiming to link the Old Town and the Castle more closely with the entire expansive urban agglomeration.

"Originally, the text pertaining to the history of Warsaw was to be written together with Professor Aleksander Gieysztor. The very conception of the book emerged in the course of conversations with him. Unfortunately, grave illness made it impossible for the Professor to complete his part. I attempted to preserve the jointly devised conception; we were concerned that the album should contain, apart from a general outline of the history of Warsaw' spatial development, also a more detailed history not merely of the Old and the New Town and the Royal Castle, but also of the city centre and left-bank districts surrounding the central part of the capital, as well as a history of the right-bank district of Praga [...]

My task of preparing copious texts on the spatial structure of Warsaw was rendered possible exclusively by the research which I was able to conduct in 1983-1986 in the Institute of Art at the Polish Academy of Sciences; here, jointly with Professor Jerzy Łoziński, I edited the first part of a catalogue on Warsaw, concerning the Old Town and envisaged as part of Katalog Zabytków Sztuki w Polsce (Catalogue of Monuments of Art in Poland). Once again, I would like to pay homage to the memory of Professor Łoziński, whose experience and enormous knowledge made possible the appearance of this chapter.

Almost every author writing about the spatial history of Warsaw poses a question about the essence of the exceptional nature of this town. Warsaw is certainly unique, a feature its shares with every urban organism. Towns resemble papillary lines, which never create an identical pattern. The inimitable character of municipal space depends on numerous factors, primarily on geographic location, the relief of the terrain and the character of water drainage, alongside which the town assumed shape, just as much as upon the people who devoted their talent and labour to it, cataclysms and fortunate coincidences, and, predominantly, historical events and social determinants".

Andrzej Rottermund it was the latter which moulded the town's external appearance, its political position and social structure. This is the re-

9

Fragment of the panorama of Warsaw seen from the Praga district at the end of the sixteenth century, from Civitates orbis terrarum *by G. Braun and F. Hogenberg, Köln 1595–1618*

ason why, similarly to every large town, Warsaw remains a specific spatial and cultural system.

What is the most essential trait of the image of the present capital of Poland? The foremost factor is its location by a broad river, which on the left bank of the town creates a high escarpment, sharply descending towards the Vistula. This escarpment, together with a long series of churches, palaces and houses standing on its top, is the most characteristic and magnificent feature in the panorama of Warsaw. A factor decisive for the city's present-day character and appearance was, however, the tangle of historical events which took place in this part of Europe. Thanks to them, Warsaw changed from a small, provincial Mazovian settlement into a large European capital, which at the end of the eighteenth century aspired to the rank of one of the most magnificent cities on the Continent. The ill winds of history degraded Warsaw to the role of a peripheral city in the Russian Empire, and then, despite temporary advancement, destroyed it to such a degree that the very possibility of its continuing to fulfil the functions of a capital was put into serious doubt. Regardless of its ideological contexts, the reconstruction of Warsaw after the second world war is recognised over the world as an exceptional conservation accomplishment.

This changeable fate of Warsaw was accompanied by transformations affecting not only the area and spatial scenery of the town, but also its place in the collective memory of the Poles. Equally thorough transformations occurred among the populace, in a manner exceptional in comparison to other European metropolises. The bitter but extremely apt opinion voiced by Jerzy Waldorff claims that true Varsovians are to be found only in Powązki Cemetery.

Indubitably, the greatest values, both spatial and spiritual, are the partially preserved and partly reconstructed historical districts of the town, suffused with rich contents and referring to national tradition and the past. The Old Town complex, together with the Royal Castle, the route following Krakowskie Przedmieście, Nowy Swiat Street and Ujazdowskie Avenue, and the two authentic palace-park complexes in Łazienki and Wilanów define most vividly the unique spatial configuration and cultural image of Warsaw. An enormous asset of the Polish capital are its extensive parks and gardens. Founded from the beginning of the eighteenth century, to be cultivated and enhanced throughout the entire nineteenth and twentieth centuries, they comprise the most precious component of municipal space.

Unfortunately, the era of uniformity and standardization, which the twentieth century appears to signify throughout the world, left deep imprints on the face of Warsaw. Hence the multitude of banal and stereotype buildings erected in the housing estates and, more recently, the artistically unremarkable skyscrapers, which lend the city centre an "American" character. Seen from afar, they constitute a warning against the alarming possibility that economic success might threaten the historical fibre of the city.

View from a terrace over the exit of the W-Z (East-West) Route towards the Praga district; in the foreground to the left, the Pod Blachą Palace

Warsaw did not exist prior to the year 1300. The landscape of the environs of the future capital of Poland was dominated by forests, such as the Kampinos Forest on the left bank of the Vistula, and woodlands interspersed with fields. This was a site particularly conducive for crossing the river, and the nearby gorges constituted a natural descent. The bed of the Vistula, relatively constant in this area, created natural conditions favourable for settlement. Obviously, these were not the only conditions decisive for the selection of this terrain as a site for the localisation of the early castle-towns. The prime factor was the oldest route along the Vistula, linking the towns of Flanders, via Gdańsk and Toruń, with Halicz-Vladimir Rus' (currently in Western Ukraine) and commercial ports on the Black Sea. In addition, it was precisely in the future area of Warsaw that land and water routes merged due to the aforementioned river ford, and from the tenth to the thirteenth centuries led to a crossing of routes bearing inter-regional significance.

The origin of a more intensive settlement movement in the future region of Warsaw dates back to the tenth century, when Mazovia already lay within the borders of the state of the Gniezno Polanie; remnants of the first discovered castle-town in Jazdów originated in a period spanning from the seventh to the ninth centuries (the present-day site of the Łazienki Park). A castle-town arose in Bródno, most probably in the first half of the tenth century, followed by the slightly later settlement of Kamion, mentioned as early as in 1065. Situated on the right bank of the Vistula, it constituted an important centre of commodity exchange and included a river harbour at the river the crossing opposite the Solec settlement. This ford was a key element in the trade route between Mazovia, Sudovia and Rus'. During the thirteenth century, the above-mentioned castle-town in Jazdów (seventh-ninth century) was replaced by a ducal castle-town, associated with Duke Siemowit I and his son, Konrad II. Archaeologists examining the Jazdów castle-town maintain that together with the adjacent settlement (suburbium) and ford (in Solec), this was the first core of early urban life in the future region of Warsaw.

The final site of the town and neighbouring ducal castle-town, however, proved not to be Jazdów, but a spot located some four kilometres further down the river. The transference of the castle-town was followed by the foundation of a town centre. Both events, of great consequence for the history of the future Polish capital, are connected with Bolesław II, Duke of Mazovia from 1294 to 1313. The latter year is the date of the first reliable source record of Warsaw as a centre containing the ducal court; at the same time, this was the year of the death of Duke Bolesław II. Eight years later, the first documentary evidence records Albert (Wojciech) Kuźma, the castellan of Warsaw.

From the very outset of their foundation, the castle-town and the city are connected with the name of "Warszowa", which during the seventeenth century was replaced by the modern form of "Warszawa". Scho-

Oak-tree — monument of nature — as old as the origin of Warsaw

VARSOVIA.

VIS

MILES POLONVS   NOBILES PO [...] LONIAE

VLA FLV VIVS

lars studying the name assume that it originated from "Warsz", presumably a knight from the Raw (Rawicz) family and the owner of a village known as Warszowa, existing probably from the turn of the twelfth century on a site corresponding to today's district of Mariensztat.

The site selected for the castle-town and city possessed exceptional qualities. It must be borne in mind that at the time the Vistula flowed at the very foot of the high escarpment, a feature which afforded excellent protection to the east and access to the river, unthreatened by floods. The nearby region abounded with numerous sources of drinking water. The flat terrain, stretching along the terrace of the escarpment, facilitated development, and its qualities were enhanced by the proximity of fertile soil, which could be cultivated. The nearby streams, flowing rapidly towards the Vistula, created the possibility of damming water, important for the purposes of mills and other technical facilities utilising water power – evidenced in the oldest panoramas of Warsaw.

The locatio of the town was performed by a group of prosperous merchants, whom Duke Bolesław brought over probably from Toruń. It is also known that from the very beginning Warsaw played a mediating role in transit trade conducted on an international scale. A distinct rise in the rank held by the town occurred during the reign of Duke Janusz the Older, who ruled over Mazovia from 1374 to 1429. He chose Warsaw as his residential seat, and in 1413 granted it the Chełmno (Külmn) town rights. This was the time of the emergence of a local group of wealthy merchants and artisans, a fact exerting an impact on the town's prosperity. From then on, its attractiveness as a place of permanent residence increased, causing the appearance of new municipal institutions and inspiring imposing architectural undertakings. The original, fourteenth-century town was wooden, surrounded by an earth-mound defences and a moat, already prior to 1339 being gradually replaced by a defensive wall and brick buildings, i. e. town gates. The climax of those undertakings was the raising of a brick collegiate church, built in two stages: before 1398 and after 1406, and a brick ducal residence, known as the Great Manor (Curia Maior), which became the nucleus of an extensive royal residence and the seat of the Sejm (Diet) of the Commonwealth. In the second half of the fifteenth century, the appearance of the first brick houses was followed by a second, outer line of walls encircling the town.

During the fourteenth and fifteenth centuries, the increased size of the population and various functions fulfilled by Warsaw expanded its terrain along the Vistula escarpment, and led to the emergence of the suburbs, one of which was situated along present-day Freta Street; the second, the so-called Czerskie suburb, was located along today's northern part of Krakowskie Przedmieście. The New Town had already come into existence at the end of the fourteenth century, but the first documentary evidence distinguishing it from the Old Town comes from 1408.

The foundation of the town was accompanied by the dividing up of the adjoining cultivated land, a process which provided a basis for the further

Panorama of Warsaw seen from the Praga district at the end of the sixteenth century, illustration from Civitates orbis terrarum *by G. Braun and F. Hogenberg, Köln 1595–1618*

16

expansion of the street network. Land belonging to the burghers was delineated by means of 150 metre-wide strips, parallel to the direction of the course of the Vistula. The fields were narrow and long, stretching from the Vistula escarpment towards the west, reaching the environs of present-day Filtrowa and Żelazna Streets, and giving rise to future streets (Swiętokrzyska, Złota, Chmielna, Nowogrodzka, Wspólna and Wilcza). The network marked by the subdivided arable land was superimposed upon that of earlier formed routes and tracts. A fragment of a tract leading towards Warsaw from Błonie was composed of the following contemporary streets: Wolska, Chłodna, Elektoralna and Senatorska. Another important tract, from Zakroczym, following the north-southern orientation, was the origin of Krakowskie Przedmieście, Nowy Swiat Street, Wiejska Street and Myśliwiecka Street.

The growth of the town and the rise of its significance accompanied the shaping of the structures of autonomous self-government in Old Warsaw. Administrative power was wielded by a hereditary wójt (elder), who in the judicature cooperated with a municipal body known as the bench. An elective self-government – the town council, headed by the mayor, already existed prior to 1376. The seat of the municipal authorities was the town hall, situated in the centre of the Old Town Market Square. The town's skyline must have been dominated by the buildings of the ducal court, located over the escarpment, as well as the towers of two brick churches: the collegiate church of St. John and the Augustine church of St. Martin. Next to them, soared the town hall tower, and further on, in the northern part of the town – the tower of the church of the Holy Virgin Mary, the New Town parish church.

Although Warsaw developed dynamically, in comparison with such towns as Cracow, Lvov, or Gdańsk it remained a relatively small centre, which even as the capital of a province could not equal castle-towns along the Baltic-Black Sea trade routes or the lines of communication between the German lands and Kievan Rus'. Even the most prosperous Warsaw families did not have at their disposal property comparable with the capital amassed by the patriciate of Cracow or Gdańsk. Good communication and favourable location could not accelerate the development of the town to a degree which would enable it to be placed on a par with the great urban centres of the Late Middle Ages. Warsaw was to owe its promotion to a considerable degree to purely political factors.

The year 1526 marked fundamental changes in the political status of Mazovia. After the death of the last Mazovian dukes, the province became part of the Crown, inaugurating the "settlement" of Polish monarchs in Warsaw, a process which lasted throughout the entire sixteenth century. King Zygmunt the Old arrived in Warsaw in 1526, and his stay in Warsaw Castle elevated its rank to that of a royal residence. Following the death of her husband, Queen Bona also settled down in Warsaw permanently, while King Zygmunt Augustus was a frequent resident.

Statue from the Column of King Zygmunt III standing on Zamkowy Square

The status of Warsaw as a capital and the further growth of the town were decided by resolutions passed at the Lublin Sejm, which assembled in August 1569, and the Convocation Sejm held in Warsaw in January 1573. The Lublin Sejm, which established a union between the Crown Lands and the Grand Duchy of Lithuania, selected Warsaw as the site for further parliamentary sessions, primarily owing to the fact that the town met suitable political conditions: it was a neutral site for Senators and Deputies from the Crown and Lithuania. Furthermore, its unquestionable asset was a central location in the Commonwealth, convenient for the representatives of the Two Nations. After the death of Zygmunt Augustus, the Convocation Sejm granted Warsaw yet another attribute to its rank by naming it the site of free elections. From the 1570s to 1655 Warsaw was the scene of 65 Diets and five elections. The transference to Warsaw of the permanent royal residence in 1596 and the King's final departure with his retinue from Wawel Castle were nothing more than consequences of earlier decisions.

Parliamentary assemblies, which lasted from several weeks to several months, gathered thousands of members of the gentry estate from all over the Commonwealth. Warsaw was obliged to provide appropriate services and accommodation for the duration of the Sejm sessions. It was also compelled to guarantee services, on a permanent basis, for the royal court, central institutions of the administrative authorities and the courts of high state officials. Those new tasks meant that the entire municipal complex underwent various changes, which entailed, primarily, the expansion of the royal residence, the erection of palaces and gentry manors, transformations in the structure of the Old Town, and a growth of municipal investments.

The economic boom merely supplemented its political counterpart. Changing courses of the most important trade routes, a phenomenon which occurred on a European scale, increased the significance of transit routes traversing Central Poland, with a special part played by the Vistula. Ensuing profits increased the prosperity of the Warsaw merchants, a fact which, in turn, created an opportunity for considerable construction investments. Particular renown in this domain was attained by the Baryczka, Giza, Korb and Strubisz families.

Large-scale trade was associated with the emergence of inns, intended mainly for foreign merchants arriving in Warsaw for parliamentary sessions and fairs. Already in 1527, King Zygmunt the Old granted the privilege of organising six annual fairs in the city. Thanks to well developed trade, both local and transit, as well as numerous gatherings of the gentry, Warsaw became a foremost centre for the bill of exchange and credit turnover in the Commonwealth.

The Warsaw patriciate comprised no more than a faction of the entire population of the town and its suburbs. The core of the Warsaw townspeople, alongside petty merchants and stall-keepers, were artisans. From 1527, when a privilege issued by Zygmunt I liquidated the dependence

Coat of arms of Warsaw on the title page in a municipal account book of Old Warsaw from 1599

of the Warsaw guilds upon Cracow, the guild organisations of the local craftsmen developed dynamically.

An important part in the life of the town was played by the Church, which, apart from cult functions, was also a centre of lively social life, playing a key role in shaping the citizens' attitudes and artistic sensitivity.

In the ecclesiastical hierarchy, Warsaw was the seat of an archdeaconry. Some of the right-bank parishes belonged to the Płock diocese, and others were part of the Poznań diocese, which also included all the left-bank parishes. The rising political status of Warsaw contributed to the arrival of monastic orders. During the reign of Zygmunt I, the existing Augustine and Bernardine orders, canons regular and Bernardine nuns were joined by the Jesuits, the Dominicans, the Bridgetin nuns and the Reformed Franciscans, under Władysław IV – by the Discalced Carmelites, the Camaldolites, the Carmelites, the Piarists, the Discalced Carmelite nuns and the Franciscans, and at the time of Jan Kazimierz – by the Knights Hospitallers of St. John, the Missionaries and the Visitant nuns.

A yardstick of the development of Warsaw during the period under examination is the size of the town population. At the beginning of the sixteenth century, Old Warsaw was inhabited by 3 600 persons, New Warsaw – by about 1 100 persons, and the suburbs – by 780 residents. All-told, the population of Warsaw totalled approximately 5 500 persons. In the first half of the seventeenth century, its size is estimated at about 8 000, taking into consideration only fully fledged citizens, who usually comprised no more than 25–28% of the total; thus, the overall number of the population reached ca. 30 000. As a rule, the Warsaw inhabitants were uniform from the viewpoint of their religious convictions, especially when after 1572 the Jewish populace was forced to move outside the limits of the town and the suburbs (upon the basis of a privilege issued to the burghers of Warsaw by Zygmunt I). Nonetheless, contrary to prohibitions, the Jews, together with other dissenters, settled down in the suburbs and, during the seventeenth and eighteenth centuries, in the private townships known as jurisdictions (*jurydyki*). Those territorial units, excluded from the influence of the municipal administration and the court system, and comprising the private property of the gentry and the clergy, were established in Old and New Warsaw, on land belonging to the Warsaw starosta, and along the banks of the Vistula: in the villages of Praga, Kamion and Golędzinów.

The city's constantly rising political role, assisted by a favourable economic boom, contributed to the reinforcement of the rank of Warsaw as a major centre for the intellectual and artistic life of the Commonwealth.

During the second half of the sixteenth century, cultural life was concentrated primarily at the court of Anna the Jagiellon, whose initiative led to the completion of a permanent bridge across the Vistula and the erection of the Ujazdów residence. The royal courts of Zygmunt

Hussar helmet, so-called kapalin (capellina), from the beginning of the seventeenth century, drawn out from the Vistula River in vicinity of Warsaw, collection of the Polish Army Museum

III, Władysław IV and Jan Kazimierz, to which scholars, poets and musicians were drawn, proved decisive also for the position of Warsaw in the country's intellectual and artistic life during the first half of the seventeenth century. The court theatre in Warsaw Castle functioned with great impetus. Numerous magnate residences and monastic orders tried to compete with the royal court. On the other hand, the participation of the burghers in the city's cultural life appeared to be more modest than in the preceding period, the sole exception being the wealthiest patriciate families, overshadowed by the comprehensive patronage of the Baryczka family.

The political, social, economic and cultural transformations which took place in Warsaw in 1579–1655 were the main factors in the city's territorial and architectonic growth. This was by no means a uniform development. The city itself remained unaltered within the defensive walls, while the suburbs, rapidly built up, experienced swift territorial expansion. The most discernible symbol of Warsaw's status as a capital was the redesigning and enlargement of its Castle, the official residence of the Monarch and the Commonwealth.

The extension of gentry and ecclesiastical property, observable in Old and New Warsaw, was equally marked in the suburbs. Alongside the sacral jurisdictions which existed outside the town walls already during the Middle Ages – Dziekania, Świętojerska and the property of the Bernardine nuns – areas belonging to monastic orders also enjoyed the status of a *jurydyka*, and new private townships continued to appear throughout the period.

Intensive municipal development spread in the southern suburb, along Suburban Market Square (a section of present-day Krakowskie Przedmieście, close to Zamkowy (Castle) Square, and in the northern suburb – along today's Mostowa Street, leading towards the bridge. Less compact development, including gentry and ecclesiastical manors, appeared along entry roads to the town (the so-called ku Świętemu Krzyżowi /to the Holy Cross/ Route – the future Krakowskie Przedmieście, Senatorska and Długa Streets).

Expanding development was restricted by bulwarks, raised in 1621-1624 to protect the town against an anticipated Turkish attack. In the subsequent years, the suburban division of land into building lots transgressed the line of the bulwarks, and adhered mainly to entry roads into the city.

The gentry's frequent gatherings during parliamentary sessions and elections, as well as enlivened commercial development produced the need for creating a new communication system across the Vistula. Since the traditional system of boat and ferry transportation was no longer sufficient, it was decided to build a permanent bridge from the extension of Mostowa Street. This first larger-scale town investment was commenced in 1568 upon the initiative of Zygmunt Augustus. The construction was continued after the death of this monarch under the aforementioned pro-

tectorate of Anna the Jagiellon, and completed in 1573. The first Warsaw bridge existed until 1603, when it was destroyed by flooding.

In about the middle of the seventeenth century almost three-quarters of suburban land belonged to the gentry and the clergy. The Warsaw landscape was defined by residences surrounded by gardens and centred around a palace or a manor, or by Church and monastic buildings, which dominated over burgher edifices and reflected the social relations prevalent in the Commonwealth as well as the functions fulfilled by the residential town of the Polish monarchs.

The wartime years of 1655–1658 led to a halt in the growth of Warsaw. In three years, the town was thrice besieged, captured and occupied by Swedish and Transylvanian armies. The hostilities damaged the Old Town and the New Town was set on fire; grievous losses were suffered in the suburbs. The devastation incurred was intensified by systematic pillage conducted by the invading troops. The Castle, other royal residences and opulent magnate residences, such as the Ossoliński and Kazanowski palaces, were looted.

The last decades of the seventeenth century marked the economic and cultural revival of Warsaw. Nonetheless, the Northern War (1700–1721) and pestilence (1708–1712) put a new halt to this process. For the town planning and architecture of Warsaw those four decades prior to renewed conflagration proved, to a considerable degree, to be decisive. The final relegation of the Old Town to a marginal status and the rising role of the suburbs determined the conditions in which the specific character of the urban agglomeration was to assume shape. The ousting of burgher property by the gentry and the Church, discernible already in the first half of the seventeenth century, became accelerated and more profound. The reasons for this phenomenon lay in the general political, economic and social conditions: the progressing decentralisation of power and the resultant increasingly strong position of the magnates, who continued to build palaces and castles in their sprawling estates, while in Warsaw they erected representative prestigious suburban residences in territory independent of the town authorities. The political rank of Warsaw fell – from 1673 the town was compelled to share the honour of a parliamentary centre with Grodno (in the Grand Duchy of Lithuania).

Serious changes also occurred in the economic life of Warsaw, which from an export centre became a centre of trade in imported commodities, thus satisfying the requirements of the royal court and magnate manors. The Warsaw crafts, restricted to production intended for the local market, were relegated to a similar position. Numerous branches of the local guilds, connected with construction, continued their activity, although even in this case the magnates incre-

Statue of King Jan III Sobieski standing on a bridge in Agrykola Street – fragment depicting the head of the monarch (see fig. 245)

23

asingly often brought over artisans from their own estates outside Warsaw. Considerable transformations affected social relations. Patrician families, for centuries associated with Warsaw, became nobilitated and abandoned the burgher estate; others, not so wealthy, left Warsaw altogether, seeking occupation in the provinces. True, we observe a "rejuvenation" of the burgher stratum, chiefly due to the immigration of new burgher families and the emergence of new fortunes — this holds true for the Wittgoff, Czamer, Loup and Riaucourt families. Nevertheless, both as regards its size and prestige, this particular stratum continued to occupy a less significant niche in the social structure of the town. To the very end of the seventeenth century, the reconstruction of the city's demographic status involved a gradual return to the state prior to the Swedish "deluge", i. e. about 18 000 inhabitants (in 1659, there were around 6 000 residents). In comparison to the first half of the seventeenth century, there occurred a distinct regression in the cultural and intellectual life of the Warsaw townspeople, due predominantly to religious intolerance and fanaticism stemming from the Counter-Reformation. Warsaw still did not have a school of higher learning, and secondary schools remained in the hands of monastic orders — the Piarists, the Jesuits and the Theatines. The role of centres of cultural life was assumed by magnatial manors and the royal court. The court of Jan III Sobieski continued the theatrical, musical and scientific traditions of its Vasa predecessor. Outstanding patrons included Stanisław Herakliusz Lubomirski and Jan Dobrogost Krasiński. Generally speaking, the urban development of Warsaw was influenced by the strong position of the magnates, independent of the King and the town authorities, as well as by the continued decline of the burghers.

Essential spatial development took place outside the boundaries of the Old and the New Town, and spread across vast areas — to Wilanów in the south, Bielany in the north, Wola in the west, and the right bank of the Vistula. The large-scale division of arable land into smaller lots occurred within the limits of former fields, and the balks separating them became roads — future urban streets. The character of the settlement movement depended on the dimension of the properties; the larger ones gave rise to spatial complexes affecting the further development of the city. The most significant development continued to take place in the *jurydyki* -jurisdictions, functioning as separate administrative units.

Alongside large spatial units, which shaped the future network of Warsaw streets, a considerable role was performed by larger residences. A spatial premise whose consequences proved to be essential for the further development of the town was the so-called Morsztyn premise, i. e. the palace and garden belonging to Jan Andrzej Morsztyn, which soon gave rise to the great Baroque layout known as the Saxon Axis.

A reconstruction of the development of suburban regions during the second half of the seventeenth century appears to be indispensable if one wishes to realise that at this time Warsaw was actually a "loosely knit complex of towns and townlets, jurisdictions and settlements, churches and monasteries, palaces and manors, landed estates, cultivated fields and orchards" (Alina Sokołowska). This collection of extensive units, not linked by means of any spatial principle, hindered the emergence of a town and determined the specific character of the town-planning of its centre. "Similarly to the jurisdictions, this was an agglomeration shaped mainly and for the gentry, reflecting the specific social-state structure of the Commonwealth, and which hampered communal urban development".

The unaltered economic and political system of the state favoured the retention of tendencies which shaped the town-planning and architectural appearance of Warsaw in the course of the entire seventeenth century. In its spatial stratum, this image became enhanced essentially by new solutions, whose ideological roots are strongly embedded within the absolutist ambitions and strivings of Augustus II. Those ambitions, effectively restricted, on the one hand, by Russia, restraining the sovereignty of Poland and, on the other hand, by the gentry, fearing political and economic reforms, attempted to find an outlet in the artistic activity pursued by the Saxon monarch. Royal plans of transforming Warsaw into a modern residential town, modelled on great European centres of power, contradicted markedly the general political and social situation in which Warsaw functioned in the first half of the eighteenth century. Despite the fact that it remained the residential town of the Polish monarchs, and that the Sejm of the Commonwealth of Two Nations continued to hold its consecutive sessions here, a fact which, at first glance, provided conditions for the maintenance of a leading role in the country, there appeared the distinct need for urgent political and economic reforms, particularly in the face of the international situation. One of the consequences of the impossibility of inaugurating such reforms was the continuation of the above mentioned spatial structure of the city, which created an obstacle for the introduction of elements of an urban economy characteristic for leading European urban centres, developing at this time. The position of the townspeople, who did not actively participate in the political life of Warsaw, was still weak; the dominating strata were the gentry and the magnates, who competed with the King. This phenomenon grew even more pronounced; as has been mentioned before, already during the previous century, old patrician families were granted noble status and abandoned the burgher estate. The economically self-sufficient magnate and gentry jurisdictions rivalled with the former commercial centre, namely, the Old Town Market Square. An important contender for municipal trade was the so-called Marywil – an architectural ensemble next to modern Teatralny Square, which, alongside a chapel and residential accommodation, contained trade facilities. Modest new pavilions surrounding the Old Town town hall, built in 1700–1701, proved poor competition in relation to the Marywil trade centre.

At the beginning of the 1760s, despite attempts at overcoming economic stagnation – certainly favoured by contacts with Saxony and the requirements of the wealthy magnates for luxury articles, as well as the revival of cultural life, caused by the almost seven year-long sojourn in War-

Teatralny (Theatre) Square, with the building of Wielki (Grand) Theatre, about 1895. Wielki Theatre was erected in 1825–1833 acc. to a project by Antonio Corazzi

25

saw of the court of Augustus III – Warsaw barely managed to attain a population of 30 000.

The political, economic and social factors characteristic for Warsaw influenced a situation in which decisive meaning for the architectural image of the town was held by the previously mentioned activity of the magnates, and for spatial development – by the undertakings pursued by the monarchs. The importance of town-planning schemes devised under Augustus II, the scale of the architecture, and the lavishness of the ornamentation were to express the ideas of absolute power and to glorify the ruler. Augustus II and the continuator of his artistic endeavours, Augustus III, aimed at the realisation of town-planning and architectural visions unique on an European scale, as evidenced in projects for the expansion of Ujazdów, Wilanów, Warsaw Castle, the Saxon Axis, Marymont and Czerniaków. Financial difficulties and, presumably, the political resistance of the gentry, who must have expressed hostility towards architecture of such a blatantly absolutist nature, were the reasons why only some of the projects were realised. Three of the new town-planning schemes: the so-called Saxon Axis, Kalwaryjska (Calvary) Route and Gwardii (Guards) Avenue, influenced the further development of the town.

The great accomplishment of the Saxon kings consisted of the introduction of a system of modern and well-organised design-construction office. The Warsaw Construction Office was headed by an outstanding architect, who coordinated and steered the work performed by architects, sculptors, and painters as well as upholsterers, cabinet-makers, stuccoers and other craftsmen. The organisation of the activity of the art department at the Saxon royal court was undoubtedly modelled on pertinent experiences of the court of Louis XIV, emulated at the time by the majority of European royal courts.

Great importance for the town planning of Warsaw was attached to the foundation of the Bielino jurisdiction (1757). Regardless of the value of the plan itself, based on the rules of classical town planning, this premise delineated the course of future Marszałkowska Street, and thus the main artery of Warsaw, which, at the time, was expanded southwards. The highly inventive owner of Bielino was Franciszek Bieliński, the Grand Crown Marshall, whose efforts were linked with the work carried out by the Pavement Committee, established in 1740, which regulated the old streets and punt in order the (open) sewage system.

The reign of Stanisław Augustus resulted in extremely dynamic development of Warsaw. In not quite thirty years, the population of the town reached 100 000 (according to certain estimates, even 150 000), and its area, within the so-called Lubomirski defences, totalled approximately 1 500 hectares (15 square km.). Warsaw reached the rank of the more than ten large European towns, whose population exceeded 100 000 inhabitants, surpassing considerably such cities in the Commonwealth as Gdańsk (36 000), Cracow (25 000) and Poznań (23 000). Despite all the encountered obstacles, Warsaw expanded rapidly into a large city. Re-

28

forms accepted at the Convocation Sejm of 1743, i. e. the activity of the Boni Ordinis Commission, did not lead to rapid changes in conditions defining both the position of the town and the manner of managing its terrains. The significance of Warsaw as a centre of both secular and ecclesiastical administration remained slight; in certain periods, the same holds true for its position as a centre of political power. Even the privilege associated with the status of the residential town of the Polish monarch countered the prestige of Warsaw, especially in an atmosphere of anti-royal moods prevalent after the first partition of Poland.

The growth of Warsaw took place in all domains of political and economic life, and followed directions indicated by projects of reforms conceived by the most enlightened members of society. Apparently, the town owed its increasingly strong position precisely to those changes which gradually affected the state system, political and social life, and, a fact worthy of additional emphasis, the cultural and scientific life of the Commonwealth. In public consciousness Warsaw was associated with the dynamic birth of wide-ranging reform aimed at, among others, the centralisation of state power and the granting of political rights to the burghers. The great leap forward, undergone in the city, also had its economic causes. It was here that a strong class of financiers, linked with the most politically active magnate milieu, took shape in the second half of the eighteenth century.

The royal court contributed to an increase in the attractiveness of the town, and thus towards strengthening its prestige. It became a strong centre of cultural and scientific life, and inspired a progressive programme of national education. Blessed with exceptional artistic taste and a comprehensive educational background, King Stanisław Augustus, well aware of the necessity of creating a new model of the Polish patriot, attracted to his court the most outstanding figures of the country. Empty land on the left-bank centre of Warsaw became filled with buildings, spreading in all directions. A considerable expansion of development took place also on the right bank of the river. As early as 1764, Stanisław Augustus purchased the vast Ujazdów estate from the Lubomirski family for the purposes of creating a palace-park complex that would fulfil the function of a royal residence. The redesigned Ujazdów Castle became a centre of a large-scale town-planning scheme, which had decisive influence on the spatial shaping of the southern part of town. Królewska (Royal) Route, parallel to former Kalwaryjska Road, was delineated in 1768–1773. An avenue leading from Ujazdów Castle and crossing Na Rozdrożu Square (the later Nowowiejska Street and Niemcewicz Street) towards Wola, as well as the extended Marszałkowska Street became a base for the spatial planning of this part of Warsaw. The dominating part of the configuration assumed the form of star-shaped circuses of the present-day Zbawiciel, Na Rozdrożu, Polytechnic and Unia Lubelska squares.

In the second half of the eighteenth century, a serious problem was posed by the situation of the Jewish population, whose number continued to grow. Although the ban on Jewish settlements in Mazovia was lifted in

Panorama of Warsaw photographed from the bank of the Praga district, end of the nineteenth century

1768, Jews were still not permitted to live in Warsaw. An attempted solution was the "Nowa Jerozolima"(New Jerusalem) settlement, established in the suburbs (the area of today's Zawisza Square), intended exclusively for Jews. Ultimately, the unrestricted settlement of Jews in Warsaw was regulated by means of decrees issued under Prussian occupation in 1799 and 1802.

In 1770, the town became encircled by a mound known as the Lubomirski defences. Its name was derived from Stanisław Lubomirski, the Grand Crown Marshal and the organiser of this scheme, which proved to be of exceptional importance for the spatial history of Warsaw. The direct reason for the earthen fortifications was fear of a plague epidemic, which swept across Poland in the autumn of that year. The bulwarks, 12,8 km. long, surrounded left-bank Warsaw by means of a wide semicircle, drawn from the Vistula, and, as has been mentioned, encompassed an area of about 1 500 hectares. "The ramparts influenced the consolidation and integration of the town area, at the same time liquidating differences between particular districts, often amassed in the course of past centuries" – wrote the historian Andrzej Zahorski in an apt characteristisation of the bulwark's importance. It should be added that these outer limits were to delineate the metropolitan area of Warsaw for almost the entire nineteenth century.

The system of municipal authorities in Warsaw remained essentially unchanged until the Sejm statute of 1791. The power of the mayor and the council continued to be restricted by the privileges enjoyed by the Warsaw starosta and the office of the Grand Crown Marshal.

A basic change in conditions hindering until then the city's spatial development and the introduction of order into urban questions was produced by the statute concerning towns, passed by the Sejm on 18 April 1791 as part of the Third May Constitution. Warsaw was no longer subjected to the jurisdiction of the starosta and the Marshal, the private townships (*jurydyki*) were liquidated, the burghers obtained full civic rights, and administrative and judicial power was to be held by a magistrate. The statute also created administrative precincts known as *cyrkuły*. Despite the failure of the Third May reforms and the loss of statehood, decisions concerning the liquidation of administrative restrictions, made in 1791, had a considerable impact on the further history of the capital.

In the wake of the third partition of Poland, Warsaw was degraded to the status of a provincial city, and ceased to act as an economic and political centre. Nonetheless, it remained the largest Polish town, with a distinguished political and cultural past, and thus continued to play a considerable role as a centre of pro-independence initiatives as well as cultural and scientific life, suffused with strong patriotic currents. The very essence of the development of Warsaw in the course of the nineteenth century was aptly described by Irena Pietrzak-Pawłowska: "The characteristic feature of the history of Warsaw after the fall of the Commonwealth was a reversal, as compared to the previous epoch, in the pattern of the interrelationship between the fate of the city and state capital. In the course of two centuries (to 1795), the functions of Warsaw as a capital city comprised the prime factor of its urban growth, in which the inner life of the city and the burghers alike was discriminated against. On the other hand, the fall of statehood led to the disappearance of the basic administrative functions of Warsaw, despite efforts aimed at their retention during the Kingdom of Poland; increasingly frequently, they became a pretext for the partitioning powers to apply assorted forms of repression. At the same time, the inner dynamic of development grew intensified under the influence of demographic growth and economic-social transformations, characteristic for the system of capitalist economy that was assuming shape on a European scale".

Years following the breakdown of the Kościuszko Insurrection and the defeat of the November Uprising signified particular political tension. Warsaw survived ten successive regimes, each of which altered the conditions for the town's development. The Prussian occupation (1796–1806) proved a time of large-scale departure of the gentry from the town, and grave limitations for the functioning of local trade and industry. The municipal area did not undergo great alterations — there being just the incorporation of small built-up edges in the western and southern areas.

Liberation from Prussian rule granted Warsaw the rank of a capital of the newly established Duchy of Warsaw (1807–1815). In 1813, its population, reduced in the preceding years, grew to almost 79 000 inhabitants.

The period of the constitutional Kingdom of Poland (1815–1830) brought realisations which considerably altered the city's appearance. It was then that the most important squares: Zamkowy, Teatralny (Theatre), Bankowy (Bank), Warecki, Trzech Krzyży (Three Crosses) and Małachowski, which to this day comprise the basic components in the city centre's urban plan, were composed. Nowy Świat, Bednarska, Żabia and Chłodna Streets underwent uniform development. A former road to the "Nowa Jerozolima" settlement was prolonged towards the Vistula (1823–1824), thus marking Jerozolimskie Avenue, one of the most important urban arteries. In several places, the area of the town was slightly enlarged, primarily in order to acquire land for the construction of new army barracks and drill grounds.

Spatial and population growth (from 81 000 inhabitants in 1815 to 145 000 in 1830) was accompanied by an expansion of industry in the city, especially textile, metal, food and leather. Factories were located predominantly in Powiśle, the western districts and Marymont. The years 1815–1830 were also a period of the transformation of former villages and settlements — future districts of Warsaw — into suburbs (Wola, Czyste, Sielce, Kamionek, Targówek, Nowe Bródno, Pelcowizna, Mokotów and Grochów).

The social structure of Warsaw also changed. Alongside the dominating burghers there appeared the middling intelligentsia, while the working class continued to grow. Great importance for the life of the town was at-

33

Photographs showing scenes from the Warsaw Uprising, 1 August–2 October 1944

tached to the opening of the Royal Warsaw University (in 1816) and the Polytechnical Preparatory School (in 1826). The capital's expansion, pursued with considerable impetus, was connected with the development of modern industry and trade, and based on financial-credit institutions, such as the Land Credit Society, the Savings Society, and, after 1828, the Bank of Poland. A planned regulation of the town, the erection of hundreds of the most necessary buildings, and the introduction of municipal facilities as well as scrupulous control of private construction enterprises were rendered possible by the creation of an effectively working administrative system. Power was wielded by the Municipal Office, supervised by the Government Commission for Internal Affairs and the Police, which oversaw the Building Office.

Planned spatial organisation was to endow Warsaw with the appearance of a modern European metropolis, and the architectonic elements of this programme constituted an important visual measure of political propaganda. The monumental elevations of government edifices and schematically designed facades of houses belonging to wealthy townspeople emulated traditional Classicist patterns – this tendency was a specific expression of the ideological compromise of the patrons, who perceived the future of Poland not in armed uprisings, but in loyal cooperation with the partitioning power. The authorities found it necessary to protect Warsaw against civil war, insurrection and revolution. The basic components of such a town-planning conception included a wide street, in which it would be difficult to build barricades, a vast square, which would enable the safe concentration of troops, and easy communication with barracks situated on the outskirts of the city. The November Uprising did not demonstrate fully the strategic assets of a city planned in this way, but they became distinct during the events that took place in the streets of Warsaw in 1861–1863.

In the wake of the November Uprising, the tsarist partitioner the past should be forgotten and that Warsaw become yet another ordinary provincial city functioning as the administration seat of a Russian *gubernia*. The authorities embarked upon the liquidation of all institutions which granted the rank of a scientific and cultural centre – primarily Warsaw University – and initiated the Russification of Warsaw by adapting certain churches to serve the Russian Orthodox rite. The ensuing political and economic repressions hindered urbanisation. This trend was reflected in the diminished population, whose number dropped to 114 000. Grave consequences for the spatial development of Warsaw were generated by the construction of a citadel at the northern end of the town (1832–1836). The Alexander Citadel absorbed the entire developing district of Fawory, and put a halt to a natural tendency towards development along the Vistula; now, development turned towards the west and the south-west: Ochota, Wola and Mokotów. Unfavourable physiographic conditions were not conducive for southward spatial development, on terrains below the escarpment. Beyond the limits of Solec, where the

Vistula became isolated from the town, there remained an extensive region unprotected against the annual floodwater. The unregulated bed of the Vistula and the Ujazdów-Łazienki park complex rendered difficult all development of terrains on the Vistula. As a result, the river banks, which, as in other European capitals could have become a representative fragment of the town, to have remained largely undeveloped up to this very day.

Urban development was continued despite temporary halts and obstacles created by the tsarist authorities. Urban development spread mainly towards the south and the west, still within the bounds of the former Lubomirski bulwarks. Generally speaking, in 1833–1864, building permissions issued for the erection of houses pertained to about 2 500 objects, the majority being brick constructions. In 1860–1864, a bridge for pedestrians and vehicular traffic was built according to a project by Stanisław Kierbedź. Its iron, latticed construction became a characteristic feature of the Warsaw landscape during the second half of the nineteenth century.

Despite the post-Uprising repressions, the Paskevich epoch and successive periods created in the economy, and especially the finances, a situation favourable for the cumulation of capital, which, in turn, consolidated the Warsaw bourgeoisie. Its representatives proved willing to work with the tsarist authorities, profiting from the extremely favourable geographic location of Warsaw, both from the viewpoint of international trade exchange (the abolition of customs barriers between the Kingdom of Poland and Russia in 1851) and the rapid development of industry and technology.

A prominent role in the economic promotion of the town and the shaping of its metropolitan space was played by the construction and subsequent expansion of the Warsaw railway junction, which granted permanence to the east-west line of the town's growth. The railway routes concentrated industrial enterprises, which, in turn, led to the emergence of industrial districts located in those regions. The first line, the Warsaw-Vienna railway, dates back to 1839–1848, entering the city from the west. In 1862, the St. Petersburg line reached the Praga district, resulting in the erection of the St. Petersburg (now: Wileński /Vilnius/) railway station in Wileńska Street.

A great achievement of the municipal authorities was the improvement of the city's communal services. In 1853–1855, Henryk Marconi opened the first municipal water supply system, encompassing part of the city centre. After 1836, the urban skyline included characteristic towers of a professional fire brigade, the first to be organised in Warsaw.

The fifty-year period from the defeat of the January Uprising to the outbreak of the first world war was a time of the extremely dynamic demographic and economic growth of Warsaw, which in the second half of the nineteenth century and at the beginning of the twentieth century, and despite political degradation, played an important international role as an economic centre in East-West trade relations. This role was partially the outcome of a concentration of the boards of great enterprises and prospe-

Photographs by L. Sempoliński and J. Bułhak of fragments of Warsaw devastated during the second world war

ring Polish and foreign banks as well as the high rank of Warsaw industry. In 1913, 595 local factories employed 41 500 workers. Prior to the outbreak of the first world war, the number of inhabitants rose to 885 000, in comparison with 244 000 after the collapse of the January Uprising. "Almost everything which was accomplished in Warsaw in the course of those fifty years in the domain of expansion, the improvement of living conditions, and the political and cultural activeness of the inhabitants was achieved in a struggle waged against official factors, a battle conducted by means both legal and illegal ", wrote Stefan Kieniewicz.

Taking into consideration the political situation of the town, this growth was exceptional. Warsaw reached eighth place among European towns as regards the size of its population, becoming, next to Berlin and Budapest, the most vital urban centre in this part of Europe. Moreover, it decidedly preceded all other large Polish towns. On the eve of the first world war, the population of Warsaw was four times larger than that of Vilno and Lvov, and five times larger than the population of Cracow and Poznań. This rise, unprecedented in Europe, took place in a territorial area only slightly different from the area delineated during the reign of King Stanisław Augustus.

During the 1880s, in the face of growing international tensions, the tsarist authorities had surrounded Warsaw with a ring of forts, in this manner finally halting the spatial development of the town beyond the line of fortifications. As a consequence, they intensified the development of all empty land within the city through the division of gardens and certain larger municipal lots. A slight increase in the size of Warsaw was associated with the liquidation of the former Lubomirski bulwarks (1875) and the inclusion into the town of the Powązki and Jewish cemeteries (1889).

In the Praga district, the lands belonging to the St. Petersburg and Terespol railways were incorporated in such a way that the town boundaries to the north and the east ran along the railway line. A further considerable expansion of the Warsaw railway junction included the completion of the Terespol (today: Wschodni /Eastern/ station (1867), reached by Kijowska Street; in 1877, its successor was the Vistula line station. The first railway bridge across the Vistula was built in 1873–1875. The dynamic and extensive growth of the Praga district was partially the outcome of a policy pursued by the tsarist authorities, who wished to link the town even more directly with the eastern parts of the Kingdom of Poland.

A prominent impact on the further spatial history of the Powiśle district and part of Praga was exerted by the construction of a bridge and a viaduct, subsequently named after Prince Józef Poniatowski (1904–1912). The new investments facilitated contact between the southern districts of Warsaw and the centre of Praga, and animated the development of southern terrains on the right bank of the Vistula.

The further expansion of the sewer and water supply network dated back to 1833, and was conducted according to projects by the English engineers William and William Herlein Lindley. A regular network of horsedrawn trams was introduced in 1882–1883. Up to the end of the nineteenth century, the town streets were lit with gas, and in 1905 the number of gas lanterns totalled more than 8 000. The electrification of Warsaw was inaugurated in 1902, the municipal power plant being built on the Vistula, in the region of Leszczyńska Street, while the tram power plant, which functioned from 1907, was situated in Przyokopowa Street. The first telephone exchange (800 users) was opened in 1881.

The character of individual central-Warsaw districts took shape in the second half of the nineteenth century. The centre was composed of Marszałkowska Street, Jerozolimskie Avenue and the side streets of those two arteries. Ujazdowskie Avenue, Szuch Avenue, Piękna Street, Matejko Street, Róże Avenue and Szopen (Chopin) Street formed an elegant district of the aristocracy and the wealthiest members of the bourgeoisie. The moderately wealthy middle classes lived mainly in the side streets of Marszałkowska Street and in the region of Elektoralna and Leszno Streets. Larger industrial enterprises were situated in the Wola, Powiśle and Praga districts. The Jewish population was concentrated predominantly in the districts of north-western Warsaw. Built-up areas beyond the town limits still preserved a semi-rural character.

The prestige of a strong capitalist economic centre, which Warsaw enjoyed at the turn of the nineteenth century, required primarily representative public utility buildings. They were erected in assorted parts of the town centre, a fact which did not favour the creation of a representative urban centre, characteristic for large European capitals.

Warsaw began fulfilling its functions as a capital before it even received them officially, an event which took place in the autumn of 1918. The Provisional Council of State existed as early as in 1916, followed by a Regency Council and the cabinets established by it — embryos of future state authority. At this time, the Municipal Council of the Capital City of Warsaw, as well as numerous institutions, important for scientific, cultural, social and professional life, inaugurated their activity. Schools of higher learning, libraries, theatres, museums and the Philharmonic were re-established and opened. A decree issued in 1916 by H. Besseler, Governor-General of Warsaw, incorporated vast suburban areas into the municipal area. In the south, they included the parish of Mokotów as well as Czerniaków and Siekierki from the parish of Wilanów; in the south-west — the parish of Czyste, and part of Żoliborz and the localities of Młociny, Kaskada, Marymont, Potok and Powązki from the parish of Młociny. On the right bank of the Vistula, the newly incorporated areas of Warsaw included Pelcowizna, Nowe Bródno, Ustronie, Utrata and Targówek (all from the parish of Bródno), as well as Grochów I, Grochów II and Kępa Gocławska from the parish of Wawer. The territory of Warsaw was subsequently further expanded in 1930, when the newly incorporated territories included Bielański Wood, and in 1938, when Służew and Służewiec were added to the capital. Generally speaking, in 1938, the area of Warsaw (without the Vistula) totalled almost 135 square km. (left-bank War-

Marszałkowska Residential District, 1950–1952, statues:
Mason and *Miner*

saw occupied almost 92 square km.). In comparison with 1913 this was an almost fourfold territorial growth. The number of inhabitants also increased considerably – from 758 400 in 1918 to 1 289 500 on the eve of the second world war.

After the regaining of independence in 1918, Warsaw started to fulfil the official functions of the capital of a reborn state. Further concentration of political, economic and state administrative centres took place. The town became the most important centre of intellectual and cultural life in the country, and constituted a distinct unit of state administration, with the status of a voivodeship. Administratively, it was supervised by a central-state administrative authority, and in its capacity as an urban organism it possessed its own self-government – an elective Municipal Council and a Municipal Board, headed by a President (i. e. Mayor).

The restitution of independence was followed by the implementation of a town-planning project which took into consideration new municipal boundaries. The only realised fragment of this widely outlined project was to be the improvement of railway communication in the City by the introduction of a cross-town line following a trench and a tunnel parallel to Jerozolimskie Avenue (1923–1933), and the construction of the so-called third (cross-town) railway bridge. The consequence of these investments was the initiation of the raising of the modern Central railway station, located in the very heart of Warsaw.

Plans for the regulation of the capital were supplemented in 1923–1926, an undertaking which entailed the delineation of Niepodległość (Independence) Avenue, the extension of Bonifraterska Street, and the construction of a railway viaduct next to the Gdańsk station. One of the most important and effective spatial realisations was the delineation of Żwirko and Wigura Avenue.

Territorial expansion, a rising population and the functional division of the town required a rapid development of a municipally run communication system, primarily bus and tram (the length of the tram lines in 1918 comprised more than 42 km., and by 1939 was almost three times greater). New avant-garde conceptions of housing estates are exemplified by the Warsaw Housing Cooperative in Żoliborz. Prior to 1939, Warsaw was a socially differentiated town, with the majority of the population composed of the working class. This differentiation becomes most obvious in the housing situation: the living conditions of the prosperous population were satisfactory, while those of the poorer strata deteriorated constantly. The growth of the population was marked in the industrial districts, already overpopulated and neglected as regards water, electricity and gas supplies as well as the sewer system. Such was the situation in Bródno, Pelcowizna, Targówek and Wola. Attempts at resolving urgent housing problems were made predominantly during periods of the favourable economic boom in 1925–1929 and 1934–1939.

The 1920s deprived the City of its primarily residential functions. Housing now developed mainly in the suburbs, contributing to a rapid urbanisation of areas recently incorporated into the town; this being the case especially in Żoliborz, Ochota and Mokotów.

Monumental government, bank and public utility buildings, together with residential housing built during the inter-war period, merged into the fibre of the main arteries, endowing the Warsaw landscape with essential symptoms of modern design, symbolically expressed by the first Warsaw "skyscraper" – the sixteen-storey "Prudential" building (1931–1933) in today's Powstańców Warszawy (Warsaw Insurgents') Square. In about 1925, the city's architectural image included solutions inspired by the most recent accomplishment of the European avant-garde. Functional architecture was closely connected with the social programme of the conception of a small flat. The ensuing quest for solutions gave rise to the above-mentioned housing estates, whose visual and spatial qualities make it possible to recognise them as the most outstanding achievements of the inter-war architectural milieu in Warsaw.

The second world war incurred extremely serious losses, only partially caused by combat; the major part of the damage resulted from a campaign of "razing the town to the ground", planned and intentionally conducted by the Nazi occupant. In September 1939, some 12% of the town was destroyed. A similar percentage of damage was the result of the annihilation of the Warsaw ghetto in April 1943. The greatest devastation, estimated at almost 58%, was incurred during and after the Warsaw Uprising, due especially to systematic arson and destruction conducted in the wake of the Uprising, from 1 October 1944 to January 1945. The majority of the devastation consisted of setting fire to the buildings. Fortunately, a considerable part of the facades and spatial structure survived; in many cases, the outer decoration of the elevation was preserved almost untouched.

The reconstruction of Warsaw was initiated immediately after combat ended. The local milieu of architects and town planners was well prepared for embarking upon this venture since several reconstruction studios had been set up in semi-clandestine and semi-legal architectural-town-planning ateliers and underground workshops. Decisions of enormous importance for the future of the town were made in the winter of 1945; they included a statute on the recognition of Warsaw as the capital of the Polish state and the establishment of the Bureau for the Reconstruction of the Capital. A decree about turning terrains in the capital into communal property, an act that was to bear enormous consequences in the future, signified the confiscation of all previous owners of their real estate. The intention of this illegal decision was to create conditions conducive, predominantly, for building a new town which would correspond not only to contemporary architectural and town-planning conceptions, but also to an ideological doctrine, proclaimed by the new authorities. Apparently, ideological arguments, on a par with aesthetic ones, were the reason for the resolution to demolish the majority of the burnt-out buildings, some of which could have been salvaged. In this manner, en-

tire quarters of nineteenth-century and early twentieth-century development were ruined.

New town-planning projects were subjected to constant modification, and their range included not only the City, but also the closest environs of the capital. Such plans placed emphasis on merging areas that would fulfil related functions, and the separation of those whose functions and principles conflicted. Thus, the city centre was to become a district of state administration and services, while the residential districts were to be shifted further from the town centre. It was decided to locate all industry in Wola, Kamionek and Żerań. Many of those premises were subsequently introduced in the course of the reconstruction and expansion of the capital.

For Warsaw, this first period, from 1945 to 1947, proved of essential significance. Work was initiated on setting into motion the water-supply and sewer facilities, indispensable for the normal functioning of any large town, the reconstruction of the Poniatowski Bridge, and the restoration of communication. The rebuilding of some of the burnt-out residential housing was commenced. The realisation of those tasks was to be assisted by the newly established Workers' Estates Foundation (ZOR). The communication network was expanded, and the most important undertakings of the period included the laying out of present-day Władysław Anders Street through the ghetto rubble and the construction of the W–Z (East-West) Route, opened in 1949, soon to become the most prominent road link connecting Warsaw and the Praga district.

The end of the 1940s witnessed the reconstruction of historical complexes, an undertaking unprecedented in the history of the protection of historical urban centres. This campaign encompassed historical monuments of the Old and the New Towns, the region of Krakowskie Przedmieście, Nowy Swiat Street and Ujazdowskie Avenue as well as Długa, Miodowa and Senatorska Streets. Once again the panorama of the Old Town, seen from the Vistula, the palaces and churches situated along the escarpment, the picturesque fragments of Krakowskie Przedmieście or Ujazdowskie Avenue with its elegant palaces and villas, became the most magnificent sections of the town. In this manner, the centre of the capital retained its unique, individual nature. This resurrection of Warsaw monuments was completed by the reconstruction of the Royal Castle and Ujazdowski (Ujazdów) Castle, which always comprised prominent elements in the town panorama.

The beginning of the 1950s introduced considerable corrections into the initiated realization of a plan for the reconstruction of Warsaw. Now, the formulation of directives for the future development of the town was also influenced, alongside political and economic premises, by elements of the doctrine of socialist realism. Great emphasis was placed on the expansion of industry and a representative shaping of the city's architectural appearance. Residential housing was relegated to the background. Another decision concerned building an underground system.

In 1951, the area of Warsaw was enlarged by the incorporation of among other districts Bemowo, Jelonki, Wawrzyszew, Chomiczówka,

Młociny, Okęcie, Włochy, Powsin, Natolin, Ursynów and Wilanów, and, on the Praga bank of the Vistula, Wawer, Anin, Międzylesie, Radość, Falenica, Miedzeszyn, Żerań, Tarchomin and Stare Bródno. Alltold, in 1951, the town, without the Vistula, totalled 41 173 hectares (422,7 square km.). The outlines of the so-called six-year plan and the ideological premises of socialist realism, albeit not fully implemented, as exemplified by the halt to the construction of the underground, left a distinct imprint on the spatial development of Warsaw and its general image. Alongside traditional industrial districts, such as Wola or Targówek, there appeared new ones – Żerań and Służewiec. The localisation of certain industrial enterprises, such as the Warsaw Steel Plant, was a serious error in spatial planning, and hindered the development of the town along the Vistula, cutting it off from Kampinos Forest, ideal for tourism and leisure, and creating a source of air pollution in considerable parts of the northern districts of Warsaw. Despite the declining tempo of residential housing, the population of the capital continued to grow, and in 1955 it reached 1 million inhabitants. The leading town-planning and architectural accomplishments of the period were represented by the so-called MDM (the Marszałkowska Residential District) and the Palace of Culture and Science. The steel construction of this largest building in the capital was a technical achievement, but the object itself left an irreversible imprint on the shaping of the city skyline. Furthermore, it introduced an element alien both to the scale and the artistic tradition of Warsaw.

An assessment of spatial and architectural solutions from the period of socialist realism should emphasise the fact that apart from their indubitable functional faults and ideologically-tainted aesthetics, the newly built estates were skillfully combined with the spatial structure of the town, the building sites were rationally utilised, and the good traditions of Polish crafts cultivated.

Socialist realism was sharply criticised during the aftermath of the political changes of 1956. This holds true also for the town planning and architecture of Warsaw. The resultant discussion produced an extensive town-planning and architectural programme, focusing on the year 2000. Nonetheless, also this plan, confirmed as late as July 1969, proved to be only partially useful, and remained unrealised due to economic difficulties, divergences between actual possibilities and theoretical premises, and administrative obstacles. The approved plan was subjected to consecutive changes; its final edition appeared in 1975, coinciding with the administrative reform of the country. The creation of the Warsaw capital voivodeship abolished administrative barriers separating the area of Great Warsaw from the former voivodeship.

Little was realised of the extremely widely conceived project. Nevertheless, accomplishments from the 1970–1980 period altered seriously the city's image, owing to the reconstruction of the Royal Castle, the building of communication routes, such as, above all, Łazienkowska Route and Wisłostrada, as well as public utility objects, such as the Central railway

station. Work on the Toruń Route, which was to link Bródno, Żerań and Tarchomin with Żoliborz, Wola and Ochota, was continued. Part of this undertaking involved the completion of the General Grot-Rowecki Bridge across the Vistula.

A new image of Warsaw took shape in 1945–1989. Its characteristic element became the monotonous housing estates situated around the centre. Several multi-storey skyscrapers, contrasting with the preserved nineteenth— and twentieth-century buildings, were introduced into the traditional pattern of the centre's streets. It seems worth noting that recently Warsaw conservation services have offered protection to objects from the second half of the nineteenth century and the most valuable buildings from the first half of the twentieth century, due to the fact that they constitute important accents in urban development and reduce the monotony of the schematic solutions proposed by contemporary architecture. The veritable pride of the town and, at the same time, a trait distinguishing it from hundreds of modern towns, are the above-mentioned historical parts of the capital – complexes of great architectural-spatial value: the Old Town with the Royal Castle, the New Town and the Royal Route, with adjacent Royal Łazienki. In the latest stage in the history of Warsaw town planning and architecture, and especially during the 1970s, there emerged a distinct tendency towards endowing the capital with metropolitan communication solutions, as well as a quest for a new model of housing estates, with a higher standard and designed to serve more fully the needs of the residents. Naturally, such schemes could not be implemented during the crisis of the socialist economy, i. e. the 1970s and 1980s, and in the face of a total breakdown of the previously prevailing economic system. New, at times architecturally interesting housing estates, such as Ursynów and Natolin, were built, but each year the number of completed flats declined. Work on the construction of the subway system, initiated in 1982, was delayed, and continues to falter owing to financial restrictions, while the completion of the whole route, from Kabaty to Młociny, is foreseen for the year 2004.

The post-1989 changes within the prevalent system have included separating the administrative and self-government authorities. Warsaw has been divided into eight communal districts, and the town authorities are now headed by the President of the town. Those innovations mark the beginning of an entirely new chapter in the history of Warsaw town planning and architecture. The capital has become an enormous building site. Tens of new architectural investments are becoming part of the urban landscape. Such processes create new challenges for the municipal authorities, since, on the one hand, it seems worth benefiting from the new opportunity of enriching the appearance of the capital, but, on the other hand, it is necessary to protect municipal space against mindless urban anarchy. After all, the heart of the matter lies in safeguarding the city's spatial structure against a blatant violation of qualities shaped by history. At any rate, it remains an unquestioned fact that the capital of Poland is one of those towns in Eastern Europe whose development appears to be exceptionally dynamic.

"Marriott" Hotel and offices of PLL LOT in Aleje Jerozolimskie, 1987–1991, project by Tadeusz Stefański, Jerzy Skrzypczak and Andrzej Wielobrodek

The Old Town in Warsaw was founded on a site almost unaffected by earlier settlements; as a result of which, during its locatio (laying out) it was possible to delineate a regular configuration. The realisation of the geometric plan was slightly deformed by the curves and refractions of communication routes as well as certain irregularities at its southern end, due to the fact that those lands belonged to the duke. The town was based on three parallel streets (present-day Piwna, Świętojańska – Nowomiejska, and Jezuicka-Krzywe Koło), along a north-south line, and perpendicular side-streets (Piekarska – Celna, Wąski Dunaj). Spatial configuration contained distinct town squares – the main square (today: the Old Town Market Square) and a market place along Dunaj (today: Szeroki Dunaj Street). The delineation of the squares and streets determined blocks intended for development whose size, in turn, defined the highly differentiated depth of the Old Town lots.

Originally, the fourteenth-century town was wooden, as was the church of St. John the Baptist, whose existence was confirmed already in 1316. It stood in the western part of the ecclesiastical plot, between present-day Świętojańska Street and Kanonia Street. An earthen defensive mound with a moat encircled the town along the line of today's inter-wall area – from the ducal castle-town in the south to the Vistula escarpment in the north-eastern part of the town. Its replacement, prior to 1339, by a defensive wall probably coincided with the time of the erection of the main town gates: the north-western Nowomiejska (New Town) and the southern Krakowska (Cracow), together with the adjoining (to the southwest) fragment of the wall (as far as today's Wąski Dunaj Street). In about the mid-fourteenth century, the defensive wall already reached the Vistula escarpment. It was also then that the brick Wielka (Great), known also as Grodzka (Town) Tower, was raised as part of the ducal castle-town.

In 1398–1406, St. John's was granted the status of a collegiate church, and became the burial site of the dukes of Mazovia. In turn, the expansion of the ducal castle led to the shaping of a spatial configuration in the area of the old castle-town and adjoining lands. The delineated entry road into the town (today: the western row of houses in Zamkowy Square) comprised a boundary between ducal and town property. To the west, there appeared ten shallow lots, later developed by the burghers, and on the side of the castle – the four lots, offered by the duke to court dignitaries and officials, were filled with manors and stables. Gradually, ducal land preceding the residence was also subdivided.

This land was granted to the Warsaw chapter. The area behind the presbytery of the collegiate church of St. John, along the defensive wall and between the two gates, became a parish cemetery – the later Kanonie open place. This was the later site of twelve residential buildings; the thirteenth, adjoining the buildings of the ducal seat (Curia Minor), housing the chancery, the library, the treasury and the archive of the collegiate church. Former ducal land was turned into Dziekania Lane and an

Barbakan (the Barbican), built in about the mid-sixteenth century acc. to a project by Giovanni Battista of Venice, reconstructed in 1953–1954

View of the Royal Castle and the Old Town seen from the Praga district

Church of St. Benon in Piesza Street in the Old Town, built in the first half of the eighteenth century; reconstructed after wartime devastation, 1957–1959

Church of the Visitation of the Holy Virgin Mary in the New Town, erected after 1411, redesigned upon numerous occasions; rebuilt after wartime damage,1947–1952 and 1956–1966

←

The Sisters of the Blessed Sacrament church of St. Casimir in the New Town Market Square, built in 1688–1692 acc. to a project by Tylman of Gameren; reconstructed after wartime damage, 1949–1955

Houses in the New Town Market Square, built in 1952–1954 and referring to Classical forms

Houses in Freta Street, built in 1951–1953 and referring to Classical forms

Dominican Church of St. Jack in Freta Street,
built in stages in 1604–1639 acc. to a project
by Giovanni Battista Trevano (?); reconstructed
after wartime devastation, 1947–1959

Paulite church of the Holy Ghost in Nowomiejska Street, erected in 1707–1717 acc. to a project by Józef Piolla; rebuilt after wartime damage, 1950–1959

Franciscan church in Zakroczymska Street, built in stages in 1679–1733 acc. to a project by Giovanni Battista Ceroni and then Józef and Jakub Fontana; reconstructed after wartime devastation, 1945–1948

The Sapieha Palace in Zakroczymska Street, erected in the first half of the eighteenth century acc. to a project by Jan Zygmunt Deybel; rebuilt after wartime damage, 1950–1955

Mostowa (Bridge) Gate, later the Gunpowder House in Rybaki Street. Originally, the gate was erected in 1582 on the bridge head, and in 1648–1649 it was redesigned into a gunpowder house

View of the New Town seen from the river; churches of the Sisters of the Blessed Sacrament, St. Benon and the Visitation of the Holy Virgin Mary

ensemble of chapter buildings. Church property also encompassed land between present-day Piwna Street and the town walls, which in 1356 Duke Siemowit III granted to the Augustine friars, brought over by him and his wife, Eufenia. An Augustine church was erected here at the end of the fourteenth century. The second area, apart from ecclesiastical property, which was not subjected to town law, was the complex of plots belonging to the Jewish kahal, situated along the southern side of Wąski Dunaj Street, between Piwna Street and the defensive wall.

A successive expansion of the town defensive walls took place after 1379, entailing the erection of two sections of the walls and the reinforcing of the towers and rectangular bastions. They closed the circumference of the town, linking it with the ducal residence. The circumference of the wall totalled 1 200 meters and enclosed an area of more than 8,5 hectares.

The favourable situation of Warsaw at the turn of the fourteenth century was reflected in the growing density of development within the town itself and the first wooden residential houses. A typical fifteenth-century burgher house faced the street with its shorter side, and had a facade crowned with a triangular or stepped gable. A building situated deeper within the lot, combined with the main part of the house by means of a wooden porch, was intended for household purposes. During the first half of the sixteenth century, the growth of the town's population resulted in an urgent need for larger residential facilities. Attempts to resolve

View of the defensive town walls with Barbakan. Extant walls originate from the sixteenth century; large fragments were reconstructed after 1946

Barbakan, built in about the middle of the sixteenth century acc. to a project by Giovanni Battista of Venice; reconstructed after wartime devastation, 1953–1954

Statue of the Little Insurgent in Podwale Street, against the backdrop of the defensive town walls, executed by Jerzy Jarnuszkiewicz in 1983

Uniform and arm of Warsaw insurgent. Collection of the Polish Army Museum

this problem led either to expanding houses further into the plots, or the building of an additional storey, to create a total of three or four. The houses also received more lavish elevations and decorative portals, while their interiors were frequently richly painted.

A second outer ring of walls, surrounding the town from the southwest, the north and the west, was raised between the mid-fifteenth and the beginning of the sixteenth centuries. This line of walls started from the spot which at the beginning of the seventeenth century became the site of the western wing of Warsaw Castle (its southern corner) – from Kamienne Schodki Street, where it joined the inner wall. Since the distance between the walls ranged from between 9 and 14 metres, there appeared an inter-mural area. A moat (probably dry) was situated immediately beyond the outer wall. Some 12 or 13 semicircular bastions were erected within the sequence of the walls, and the gates proper were preceded by foregates. The final element in the mediaeval expansion of the walls was the erection of the Barbican in front of Nowomiejska Gate (1548).

From the end of the fourteenth century, the Old Town possessed a suburb in the form of the New Town. The shaping of its configuration progressed along a route leading to Zakroczym; the development next to it became the western row of houses in the market square. To the north, the New Town was enclosed by a stream flowing along today's Wójtowska Street, and to the east – by the Vistula escarpment. The parish church of the Holy Virgin Mary, situated in the northern part, at the edge of the escarpment, was founded by Duke Janusz the Older and his wife, Anna Danuta. Originally built in about 1409, it continued being expanded to 1497. The church stood next to a hospital, a school and the residence of the parish priest. The residential houses of the New Town were wooden, as was the town hall.

The lands located in direct proximity to the New Town, and not subject to municipal judicial authority, belonged to the canons regular. This area started at the western side of present-day Koźla Street and followed a narrow strip between today's Świętojerska, Franciszkańska and Anielewicz (formerly: Gęsia) streets to the very boundary with Wola. The property of the canons adjoined the building plots of the New Town, stretching to the north, together with Wygon, land belonging to *the wójt* and the hospital of the Holy Ghost. The centre of these lands was the non-extant church of St. George (Polish: Jerzy, hence the name of the street: Świętojerska), built before 1339 and founded by Duke Bolesław IV and his mother, Anna, Duchess of Mazovia.

In the course of the seventeenth century, development in the Old Town underwent various transformations, but it remained territorially restricted by the line of the defensive walls. Relatively speaking, the most considerable changes took place in the north-eastern part of the Old Town, as well as in the southern bloc next to the market square, where from the year 1597 plots were purchased for the purposes of constructing a Jesuit church and monastery (the area between Jezuicka and Świętojańska streets, along

Fragment of housing in Krzywe Koło Street in the Old Town

The Old Town Market Square,
the Barss (eastern) side

⟶

The Old Town Market Square,
the Kołłątaj (western) side

⟶

The Old Town Market Square, open-air summer cafes at the junction of the Dekert (northern) and Barss (eastern) sides

←

The Old Town Market Square, salesmen of paintings against the background of houses along the Barss (eastern) side

←

House at the corner of Zapiecek Street and the Old Town Market Square with a clock installed during reconstruction in 1952–1953

→

Kanonia Street in the Old Town

→

Jesuit church of the Immaculate Conception of the Most Holy Virgin Mary of Mercy in Świętojańska Street, built in stages in 1598 and 1608–1620; reconstructed after wartime damage, 1948–1957

→

the lane next to the collegiate church). Land occupied by burgher houses increased slightly along the two main entrances into the town: the Nowomiejska and the Krakowska gates, which in the first half of the seventeenth century became densely built up with burgher houses. Further modification occurred also in elements of the town walls (e. g. Poboczna /Side /Gate was created in 1598–1617 along the prolongation of Wąski Dunaj Street). Other alterations were limited to the addition of a storey or two to the burgher houses and the redesigning of the town hall (after 1580); the town hall tower became an important accent in the city panorama. A fire which broke out in 1607 had grave consequences for the appearance of the Old Town, and made it necessary to rebuild numerous burgher houses, which, consequently, assumed new architectural forms. In the first half of the seventeenth century, new developments in the town panorama included the powerful outline of the Castle, the newly erected Jesuit church and the Baroque facades of the St. John and Augustine churches.

The landscape of New Warsaw differed considerably from the Old Town. As has been mentioned, it was dominated by wooden houses, rather sparsely scattered among gardens and orchards. Blocs of compact development were concentrated in the Market Square, with a town hall in the middle, and along part of Zakroczymska and Freta streets. The church of the Holy Virgin Mary, redesigned in the second half of the sixteenth century, continued to be a dominating accent in the panorama. The end of that century and the first half of the seventeenth century witnessed the buying out of burgher plots by the gentry, whose representatives erected manors or residential houses, intended chiefly for courtiers and servants.

More prominent changes occurred in the Old Town after 1657, when Warsaw was recovering from the Swedish "deluge". The last reserves of land between the defensive walls were put to use, and the development of the lots grew denser. This period also marked an end to the transformations of the functional and spatial configuration of the Old Town houses. Such buildings were composed of a frontal house facing the street, with a courtyard behind and out-building, with a passage hallway, facing the rear street, permitting vehicular access. The height of the front building was established as three or four storeys. The accepted spatial configuration of the houses, with an inner staircase, required the introduction of an additional storey above the top floor including a skylight – the so-called lantern to illuminate the stairs. Such lanterns became a characteristic element in the panorama of the Old Town in Warsaw. At the same time, the transformation of single-family houses into tenement houses was becoming more intense.

Concerned about the appearance of the immediate surrounding of the Castle, King Jan III Sobieski established a commission whose task was to put the square before Krakowska Gate into order. In 1684, the Gate itself was redesigned upon his initiative.

During the reign of Stanisław Augustus, the Old Town, which had ceased to be the central district of Warsaw, attracting predominantly arti-

Zapiecek

EXCHANGE

1953

RYNEK STAREGO MIASTA.
POMNIK
KVLTVRY NARODOWEJ
I WALK REWOLVCYJNYCH
LVDV WARSZAWY
ZWALONY W GRVZY PRZEZ
FASZYSTOWSKICH OKVPANTOW
W 1944 ROKV
RZAD POLSKI LVDOWEJ
Z RVIN PODZWIGNAL
I NARODOWI PRZYWROCIL
W LATACH 1951-1953

KANTOR NA POCZCIE

POCZTA POLSKA
URZAD POCZTOWY
WARSZAWA 40

sans, with a population which had grown from 5 000 in the middle of the century to almost 11 000 in 1792. Since space for new houses was no longer available, additional storeys were built onto old houses and the last wooden edifices were pulled down, to be replaced by brick houses. The town walls were almost entirely rebuilt.

At this time, important changes were also introduced in the New Town, where, alongside the still considerable number of wooden manors (56% of the total), brick objects were raised in the Market Square and in Freta, Przyrynek, Swiętojerska and Franciszkańska streets. Almost one-quarter of the 11 000 inhabitants were craftsmen.

In about the mid-eighteenth century, land adjoining the New Town and located in Swiętojerska, Franciszkańska, Bonifraterska, Wygon and Nalewki streets as well as in Wałowa and Koźla lanes were divided into building plots.

Despite numerous attempts at its liquidation, Gnojna Góra (Dung Hill), the town refuse dump, located in close proximity to the Castle, continued to function. The municipal water supply was relatively efficient — the old ducts, which from the Middle Ages provided water to the market squares of the Old and the New Town, remained in use.

At the time of Stanisław Augustus, the Old Town was the scene of the most significant acts of ceremonial court life. During coronations, the procession route led from the Castle to the collegiate church of St. John along Swiętojańska Street by means of a so-called bridge over the street, covered with red cloth. In turn, the Old Town Market Square served as a backdrop for the ceremonial knighting of cavaliers of the Golden Spur, performed during the second day of the coronation. Processions held on Corpus Christi, always attended by the monarch, followed a route along the streets of the Old Town.

In the wake of the partitions of Poland, under Prussian rule, the defensive walls of Old Warsaw were pulled down and the Nowomiejska and the Poboczna gates were raised; Krakowska Gate was demolished during the years of the Duchy of Warsaw.

Larger-scale regulation was conducted during the Kingdom of Poland. In 1818–1821, Jakub Kubicki pulled down fragments of buildings situated in front of the western facade of the Castle, in this way creating Zamkowy Square, whose shape resembled its present-day counterpart.

The activity pursued by the Society of Care for Monuments of the Past during the early decades of the twentieth century proved particularly important for the Old Town. Established in 1906, the Society attracted architects, artists, conservators, historians, art historians, lovers of historical monuments and collectors. Its undertakings (pursued until 1944) contributed to the protection of the Old Town houses, including the Fukier and Baryczka houses, and to salvaging remnants of the defensive walls. In 1912, the Society had moved away the market from the Old Town Market Square. In 1928–1929, it executed new polychrome facades on a majority of the Market Square houses; the authors were outstan-

View of the tower of the (former Augustine) church of St. Martin. The original church was erected after the first half of the fourteenth century, and later expanded and redesigned upon numerous occasions, together with the façade after 1744 acc. to a project by Karol Bay; rebuilt after wartime devastation, 1949–1962

←————————

Building of a gate leading from the Castle to Kanonia Street, erected in about 1620; reconstructed after wartime damage, 1962–1963

←————————

Swiętojańska Street, seen from Zamkowy (Castle) Square towards the Old Town Market Square

————————→

ding Polish painters – Felicjan Szczęsny Kowarski, Wacław Borowski, Zofia Stryjeńska, Zbigniew Pronaszko, Edward Kun, Tadeusz Gronowski, Leonard Pękalski and Ludomir Slendziński. Notwithstanding the conservation, the status of the Old Town remained unchanged: the district was still inhabited by poor families, living in crowded and unsatisfactory sanitary conditions.

The centuries-old history of the Old and the New Town came to an end during the Warsaw Uprising of 1944. Despite the fact that as a result of an unfavourable development of the events, neither the Old or the New Town were assigned a foremost role in the strategic plans of the Uprising, the insurgent detachments withdrew into the region of the Old Town. On the day of the outbreak of the Uprising, this area was part of the First Region of the Home Army "City" District, and, subsequently, of the "North" Group, under the command of Colonel J. K. Ziemski "Wachnowski". In the Old Town, intensified attacks started on 17 August 1944, when the line of the front was located near Bonifraterska Street. From that day to 2 September, when decimated insurgent detachments ended their evacuation by means of sewers leading to the city centre, the Old Town remained the target of incessant attack, from both air and land. In battles waged in the streets the Germans employed their best and most modern equipment; they also resorted to cruel deceit, such as tanks filled with explosives, which they abandoned in Piwna Street on 13 August. The unaware insurgents moved the tank-trap to Piekarska Street, where it exploded, killing hundreds among the gathered crowd. Extremely heavy battles were conducted in the Royal Castle, whose northern wing and part of the western wing facing Świętojańska Street were destroyed completely. In turn, the ruined St. John's cathedral became the site of fierce battles waged from 25 to 30 August. Ultimately, on 30 August, German detachments reached the New Town Market Square. Now the insurgents could attempt to make their way across the enemy lines, surrounding the Old and the New Town. Unfortunately, those attempts ended in a fiasco; the only possible solution was to withdraw from this region *via* the sewers. More than two weeks of combat almost totally destroyed the Old and the New Town. Historians dealing with the Warsaw Uprising maintain that the defence of both those districts was the most horrific episode in the Uprising.

The realisation of the postwar decision to rebuild the New and the Old Towns was preceded by the removal of rubble and the preparing of inventories of the ruins. Detailed architectural research was conducted and thorough project studies were performed. Despite the enormous scope of the damage, the façades of certain houses (e. g. the Dekert side of the Old Town Market Square), cellars and innumerable fragments of original decoration remained preserved, providing a foundation for the total reconstruction of the devastated area. The reconstruction in question was conducted by means of assorted methods, and was based on a variety of principles. The outcome of the accepted premises was a new, uniform town

Zamkowy Square with the exit of Piwna Street

86

complex, which, despite references to the state prior to the devastation, comprised the work of a large group of architects, conservators, painters, sculptors and artists, representing numerous branches of the arts. The best preserved fragments, such as houses along the Dekert side of the Market Square or certain sections of the town defensive walls, regained their former shape by means of strictly conservationist undertakings and the introduction of relatively slight supplementation. The best example of such an approach is the majority of house frontages in the Old Town Market Square, such as the Fukier and Dukes of Mazovia houses or along the Dekert side of the Square (including the Falkiewicz, Baryczka, and the so-called Pod Murzynkiem houses). Nonetheless, most buildings were restored completely upon the basis of existing remnants, old inventories or prewar photographs, and the incorporating of preserved original elements. As a rule, reconstruction pertained to the state of the building prior to its destruction, but in many cases the restoration of certain parts was rejected, especially those originating from the second half of the nineteenth or the twentieth centuries or lacking detailed documentation. This was the rule observed during the reconstruction of houses situated beyond the Market Square, e. g. in Piwna, Swiętojańska and Nowomiejska streets. On frequent occasions, the architectural details, e. g. cornice profiles or window frames, were "improved", rendering them more classical. In the case of several objects, such as the Barbican, certain houses and, especially, the Jesuit church and the cathedral, the applied method consisted of the reconstruction of their original forms. In the instance of the Barbican, this denoted the recreation of its Late Gothic external form, together with later decorative elements (attic); a totally new solution was employed in the case of the front part of the cathedral's corpus, given a Gothic appearance and with a facade designed by Jan Zachwatowicz.

With the exception of certain quarters, the reconstruction of the houses was not extended to all buildings within the street blocks, in this way creating new, spacious courtyards. This held true predominantly for blocks along the western side of Piwna and Nowomiejska streets as well as within the entire New Town. In the majority of cases, an attempt was made to recreate only the facades, and the interiors were designed anew, sometimes only with the retention of the former pattern of the ground floor. In several houses, efforts were made to maintain remnants of sixteenth-century murals (20 Old Town Market Square and 40 Old Town Market Square) and painted ceilings (34 Old Town Market Square). Among the relatively numerous extant original portals, the most magnificent are those in the Old Town Market Square: the Pod Murzynkiem (no. 36), the Baryczka (no. 32), the Plumhoff (no. 31) and the Talenti townhouses (no. 38).

The uncovering of the defensive walls led to the liquidation of adjacent buildings, in this fashion recreating the former lanes running alongside the walls, in the form of passages for pedestrians. Finally, many houses, especially on the outskirts of the Old Town, including in Brzozowa, Ry-

Arch-cathedral of the Beheading of St. John the Baptist, originally erected about the half of the fourteenth century, later redesigned upon numerous occasions; the present-day façade acc. to a project by Jan Zachwatowicz, 1947–1956

The statue of the Mermaid, executed by Konstanty Hegel, Old Town Market Square

Old Town and the Royal Castle seen from the bell tower of the Bernardine church of St. Anne

←

The statue of the Mermaid on the Old Town defensive walls, moved to the Old Town Market Square in 2000

→

cerska or Piekarska streets, erected during the last years of the reconstruction of the Old Town, i. e. in the 1960s, or along the majority of the streets in the New Town, were built without any reference to their original shape, and only adapted to the Old or New Town development scheme as a whole. Special mention is due to the contribution made by artists and craftsmen, who outfitted the recreated buildings, especially the burgher houses, with contemporary elements of decoration – paintings, sgrafitti, sculpture, lattice work, doorposts, signboards, etc.

Professor Piotr Biegański, one of the authors of the conception of the reconstruction of the Old Town, distinguished four stages in the recreation of this historical complex. "The first – to 1947 inclusively – was devoted to the gathering of scientific material, conceptual studies and the immediate preservation of those buildings which were to be restored to their authentic condition; the second stage – to 1950 – focused on continued preservation, the reconstruction of certain objects, the preparation of a town-planning project for the historical districts, and the completion of a tunnel for the E–W thoroughfare known as the W–Z Route, as well as work on an initial project for the reconstruction of the Royal Castle and the commencement of rebuilding. The third stage – to 1955 – ended the removal of rubble from the Old Town, and initiated investigations of the now accessible ground floors and cellars, the preparation of conservation documentation and the realisation of the larger part of the development of the Old and the New Towns. The fourth stage – to 1960 – was a period of the completion of the reconstruction of all the elements of the Old Town complex, together with the defensive walls and the surrounding of the historical complex". The Old Town Market Square was completed in July 1953.

The reconstruction of the Old and the New Towns involved the most outstanding Polish conservators. The main author of the project was Mieczysław Kuzma, who supervised the work conducted in three conservation workshops, one of which he headed himself; the other two were led by Stanisław Brukalski and Piotr Biegański. The whole undertaking was directed by Professor Jan Zachwatowicz, the then Chief Conservator. Other contributors to the rebuilding of the New and the Old Towns included the architects Stanisław Żaryn, Teodor Bursze, Anna Boye-Guerquin and Wacław Podlewski, painters: Bohdan Urbanowicz, Helena and Lech Grześkiewicz, Juliusz and Helena Studnicki, Edward Burke, Jacek Sempoliński and Zofia and Roman Artymowski, as well as the sculptor Alina Szapocznikow and Henryk Grunwald, an artist working in metal.

Today, half a century after the decision to reconstruct the Old and the New Towns, it could be said with full conviction that the complex was put to suitable use, guarantees good living conditions for its residents, and constitutes an attraction for tourists from all over the world. The high level of the conservation work and the special place of this site in the history of Warsaw and the Polish nation proved decisive for the inclusion of the Old Town on the UNESCO list of world cultural heritage.

In about 1300, the dukes of Mazovia, members of the Piast dynasty, built on the high bank of the Vistula a small castle-town, the core of the future Royal Castle, soon to be expanded and linked with the newly founded town by means of fortifications. The first building, of brick and stone, was the so-called Wielka Tower, later known as Grodzka Tower, which dates back to the first half of the fourteenth century, and whose lower part has survived to this day. The lowest level of the interior of the Tower, which is particularly worthy of attention, was a prison chamber, which housed inmates sentenced by the Warsaw town court.

Several decades later, at the turn of the fifteenth century, the ducal seat was expanded upon the initiative of Duke Janusz the Elder, and a large building, which the documents describe as *Curia Maior*, was erected. Representative interiors, situated on the first storey, consisted of an extensive hallway intended for festivities and court gatherings, and a chamber used by the duke as apartments. The Mazovian Sejm convened in two large chambers on the ground floor. At the time, the level of the courtyard in front of the *Curia Maior* was much lower (about 1,5 metres), so that the present-day cellars could have comprised the ground floor. One of those interiors – particularly splendidly shaped, with a polygonal pillar supporting the vaulting – was probably the ducal treasury. The appearance of the residence is reflected not only in the ground floor interiors, but also by the facade of the Curia, facing the courtyard and reconstructed in accordance with preserved prewar inventories. The last dukes of Mazovia, Stanisław and Janusz II, died in the Curia in 1524 and 1526.

From 1569, i. e. after the signing of the Union of Lublin, which finally united Poland and Lithuania, the two nations of the Commonwealth, the Royal Castle in Warsaw became not only a monarchic residence, but also the seat of the Sejm of the Commonwealth. The "New Masonry-built Manor" was erected in 1569–1572, and the old Gothic *Curia Maior* was redesigned. The new Renaissance building was conceived by renowned Italian architects employed at the time in Poland: Giovanni Battista Quadro and Bernardo Morando, invited by King Zygmunt Augustus. The former was the author of the magnificent town hall in Poznań, and the latter – of the Renaissance architecture of Zamość. The representative first storey of the "New Manor" included eight ceremonial chambers of the royal apartment, entered by a staircase in the then round tower (today: the Władysław Tower). The most impressive part of the royal apartment was the Grand Hall, used for, among other events, ceremonial royal feasts and important audiences. From the reign of Zygmunt Augustus the ground floor consisted of court accommodation. Here was, among others, the chamber of the court dwarfs and, subsequently, the living quarters of the ladies-in-waiting of Anna of Austria, wife of Zygmunt III Vasa. (In accordance with tradition, the redesigned Royal Castle referred to the residential functions of this part of the Castle by restoring the appearance of two court quarters: one facing the Vistula and the other – the Great Courtyard). The

Eagles on the throne backrest in the Throne Room at the Royal Castle in Warsaw

Royal Castle with a bridge in the area before Krakowska (Cracow) Gate from the second half of the fifteenth century

Royal Castle, Court Rooms on the ground floor – so-called Third Chamber, 1570–1571; reconstructed in 1971–1984

Royal Castle, Court Rooms on the ground floor – so-called Main Chamber, 1570–1571; reconstructed in 1971–1984

Royal Castle, details of Zygmuntowska Tower, 1613–1619, project by Mateo Castelli

Royal Castle, Single-pillar Room on the ground floor, 1569–1572 and 1600–1604; reconstructed in 1971–1984

Royal Castle, corner turret in the eastern façade, 1613–1619, project by Mateo Castelli; reconstructed in 1971–1984

Royal Castle, former Deputies' Chamber on the ground floor, 1569–1572 and 1600—1604; reconstructed in 1971–1984

Royal Castle, Chamber and Cell in Grodzka (Town) Tower, first half of the fourteenth century and 1526–1549; reconstructed in 1971–1984

Royal Castle, Grand Stairs, 1768,
project by Jakub Fontana; reconstructed
in 1971–1984

Royal Castle, the Canaletto Room, 1776–1777, project by Domenico Merlini; reconstructed in 1971–1984

Royal Castle, the Canaletto Room, 1776–1777, project by Domenico Merlini; reconstructed in 1971–1984

Royal Castle, Chamber of the Crown Horse Guards, 1768, project by Jakub Fontana; reconstructed in 1971–1984

first floor in the former ducal *Curia Maior* contained the Great Council Hall (the Senators' Hall), while the Deputies' Chamber was situated beneath it, on the lower storey. This latter chamber was a large interior, whose vaulting was supported by three pillars placed in the middle. At the time of the parliamentary sessions held here, some 190 Deputies sat on benches surrounding the Marshal's chair. During the most recent reconstruction 32 coats of arms of the lands and voivodeships of the former Commonwealth, depicted on the vaulting, were recreated, thus restoring the symbolic meaning of the former Deputies' Chamber.

Within the range of the royal residence there existed yet another ensemble of Gothic buildings situated near the church of St. John and called, by way of contrast with *Curia Maior*, the Curia Minor. From 1536, this was the residence of Anna, daughter of Konrad III, the Duke of Mazovia, and then of Queen Bona and Anna the Jagiellon.

The great expansion of the Castle in 1600–1619 was associated with the transference of the royal residence of Zygmunt III from Cracow to Warsaw. At this time, the Castle was transformed into a magnificent edifice, whose general outline resembled the present-day one. The characteristic features of the building also originate from this period. In accordance with the premises accepted by Zygmunt III and his architects, this was an urban palace, closely connected with the town through its suitably balanced proportions and architectural accents. Similar to the alterations conducted under the last Jagiellon king, the authors of the building were Italian: Giovanni Trevano, Giacoppo Rodondo, and Matteo Castello Paolo del Corte. At the very end of the reign of Zygmunt III, the Castle received powerful fortifications facing the Vistula, introducing a new element into the town panorama as seen from the river.

A wide range of work, encompassing mainly the decoration of the Castle elevations and the outfitting of the interior, was conducted in 1637–1643, during the reign of King Władysław IV. The prime architect of this monarch was Giovanni Gisleni of Rome, who designed decorations for the Władysław Tower, the gate portals facing the Great Courtyard, and Grodzka Gate. Fortunately, it was possible to save numerous fragments of the Gisleni embellishments, which were incorporated into the present-day form of the Castle. The same projects were also used for arranging one of the most beautiful Castle interiors, the so-called Marble Room, which, albeit rather extensively redesigned under King Stanisław Augustus, makes it possible to appreciate the outstanding talent of the Roman architect.

Due to the exceptional artistic culture and subtle taste of both monarchs from the Vasa dynasty, the Royal Castle in Warsaw became one of the most impressive royal residences in Europe. Its rooms and chambers were richly outfitted and furnished. Their ceremonial character was accentuated by marble portals and floors as well as carved stone fireplaces. Particular attention was attracted by the lavishly decorated ceilings and dozens of magnificent tapestries hung on the chamber walls. At the same time, a copious theatre hall was set up in the southern wing of the Castle.

Already during the 1630s, it was used for staging plays by William Shakespeare as well as numerous ballet and opera spectacles. King Władysław IV was a great expert and lover of Italian opera, whose beginnings date back to that period.

At the time of King Jan Kazimierz, Warsaw was twice occupied by the Swedes. The Castle suffered serious losses during the Swedish invasion (1655–1656): its interior was plundered – even gilt was stripped off the wall panels.

The successive residents of the Castle, Michał Korybut and Jan III Sobieski, concentrated their efforts primarily on putting the interiors into order and adapting them to the needs of the court ceremonial, the work conducted by the Parliament and the daily life of the court.

Work was commenced on a larger scale during the reign of King Augustus II of the Saxon Wettin dynasty, elected to the throne of the Commonwealth of Two Nations in 1697. The exterior form of the Castle building was rendered uniform, a second storey being added above the Gothic part, i. e. the former *Curia Maior*, the third storey of the southern wing was removed, and Grodzka Tower was elevated. New outfitting was installed in the Senators' Hall, which at the time of Augustus II was still situated in the former *Curia Maior*, now with an additional storey. The greatest construction investment involved a new wing, built by Augustus III and facing the Vistula. This undertaking was carried out during the 1740s upon the basis of a project by Gaetano Chiaveri, an outstanding Italian architect. The Late Baroque elevation (recreated meticulously during the reconstruction of the Castle) is regarded to be one of the most outstanding achievements of European architecture from the first half of the eighteenth century; subsequently, Chiaveri became renowned as the designer of the famous Catholic church of the royal court in Dresden.

A consecutive chapter in the history of the Royal Castle in Warsaw was the reign of Stanisław Augustus Poniatowski (1764–1785), who inherited the Castle in a highly unsatisfactory condition – some of the interiors, such as the Grand Hall, being quite incomplete. This is the reason why from the very outset of his reign this monarch planned the creation of new interior decorations as well as the redesigning and expansion of the official residence. Unfortunately, none of the projects were implemented, and the King was capable of accomplishing only smaller adaptations and a new arrangement of the majority of the Castle interiors. An important episode during the first years of the reign of Stanisław Augustus was the invitation to Warsaw of Victor Louis, the young but acclaimed French architect. Despite the fact that his plans were also to remain unrealised, they exerted a strong impact on the local royal architects; it should be stressed that many of the elements designed by Louis (e. g. wall panelling, door wings and bronze objects) were made in Paris and then sent to Warsaw. In the majority of cases, they were applied to the Castle interiors during the 1770s and the 1780s. Before this occurred, however, in 1767 fire destroyed the southern wing of the Castle. The wing was rebuilt in

Royal Castle, Sanctuary of the Small Chapel, 1775–1777, project by Domenico Merlini; reconstructed in 1971–1984

Dome of the Sanctuary

Royal Castle, Old Audience Room, 1775–1777, project by Domenico Merlini

Royal Caastle, Apotheosis of the Polish Genius and Peace – Patrons of the Flourishing of the Arts, Science, Agriculture and Commerce under Stanisław Augustus, *plafond by Marcello Bacciarelli; interior reconstructed in 1971–1984*

the following year according to a design by Jakub Fontana, the leading architect of the monarch and the Commonwealth. It now contained new interiors, including a ceremonial staircase – the so-called Grand Stairs, and a Chamber of the Crown Horse Guards, serving as a guardhouse for the Castle guards keeping watch in front of the royal private apartments. At the same time, the above mentioned Marble Room was restored and partially redesigned. This ceremonial interior, which during the Vasa period was regarded as the most important, now served as a second antechamber in the state apartment; in accordance with the rules of the Warsaw court, it was here that higher rank courtiers gathered during ceremonial audiences. Jakub Fontana, who worked on this interior in 1769–1771, preserved the basic elements of the architectural composition of the old Vasa room as well as the rather unaltered lower part of the walls below the beams and the door frames. He added 22 portraits of Polish monarchs, from Bolesław the Brave to Stanisław Augustus, a plafond painted by Marcello Bacciarelli,and statutes of Justice and Peace, placed over a mirror and executed by Andre Le Brun. The room was envisaged as a place commemorating rulers on the Polish throne. Stanisław Augustus also honoured the creators of the interior: Fontana, Bacciarelli and Le Brun, by a special plaque placed in the wall.

After the death of Jakub Fontana, the position of the leading architect was assumed by the Italian Domenico Merlini. His designs were used for arranging the Royal Apartment (1772–1788), whose distinct elements include the Chapel, the Canaletto Room, the Old Audience Room and the Royal Bedroom (actually the joint work of Merlini and Fontana), all featuring excellent works of art. The character of this interior is defined by elegant wall panelling, made of yew wood, the delicate design of the upholstery and the warm hues of canvases painted by Bacciarelli. The Chapel was designed entirely by Merlini. Due to its small size, it was frequently called the Small Chapel in order to differentiate it from a chapel previously built during the Saxon period on the first storey of the new wing facing the river (today it houses the Concert Hall). From 1777, the Chapel served the King for daily religious practice, even more so considering that the aforementioned Saxon Chapel was adapted for the purposes of a court theatre. The most important religious ceremony performed in the Small Chapel was the washing of the feet of old men on Holy Thursday. The Chapel is an eloquent example of the Early Neoclassical style represented by Merlini – the elegance of the well-proportioned architecture reveals discernible traces of a Baroque approach to space and colour. The arrangement of the hues of the elements, made of green, dark red and golden stucco, was echoed in the majority of the Merlini projects.

Immediately in front of the Chapel Merlini designed one of the most beautiful interior spaces in the Castle, where he displayed paintings by the Venetian Bernardo Bellotto, showing views of Warsaw and Wilanów. Bellotto, who is known by the name of his famous uncle, Canaletto, was considered one of the most outstanding European artists of his time. In

Royal Castle, Royal Bedroom, 1772–1775, project by Jakub Fontana and Domenico Merlini, reconstructed in 1971–1984

1767, after working at the courts of the Saxon Electors in Dresden and Munich, the imperial court in Vienna and the courts of Italian dukes, he settled down permanently in Warsaw, where in Stanisław Augustus he found an enlightened patron and a demanding client. Fortunately, all the Bellotto canvases survived the war and played an important role in the reconstruction of Warsaw, frequently acting as sole evidence of the appearance of war-ravaged palaces, churches and houses. During the same period, in 1776–1777, Merlini designed the adjacent Old Audience Room, which fulfilled its titular functions until the King set up the ceremonial Throne Room in the Grand, or State Apartment. The coauthor of this Early Neoclassical interior was the painter Marcello Bacciarelli, who executed a plafond depicting *The Flourishing of the Arts, Sciences, Agriculture and Commerce under Stanisław Augustus*, supraporta paintings illustrating royal virtues: Strength, Common Sense, Faith and Justice, and portraits of the monarch's parents: Stanisław Poniatowski and Konstancja, born Czartoryska. Royal artisans produced a magnificent floor in the form of a "whirling" rosette; bronze candlesticks were purchased by the King in Paris, and the marble elements of the fireplace, together with the carved head of Hercules, were brought over from Rome. A closer analysis of the contents of the works of art featured in this room proves that they embodied a rich programme referring to the country's political and economic situation. On the one hand, he wished to elevate his own authority and prestige; hence the royal virtues and a comparison to mythical Hercules. On the other hand, the theme of the plafond portrayed the principles upon which the Polish ruler based his policy of dragging the country out of the predicament it faced at that time.

When in 1777 work was completed on the King's Royal Apartment, he immediately undertook the designing and outfitting of the Grand Apartment. The first of its chambers was the largest and an exceptionally ceremonial interior, officially known as the Grand Chamber, although owing to its assorted functions it was also called the Ballroom, the Dining Room or the Concert Room. During the reign of Stanisław Augustus, it served primarily court ceremonies. The authors of the Chamber's architectural design and interior decoration were Merlini and Jan Chrystian Kamsetzer, a young royal protégé, who improved the Merlini project considerably and completed the whole undertaking in 1781. The architects decorated the interior with assorted works of art, such as impressive candelabra; fragments of the outfitting, including door wings, were designed in 1765–1766 by Victor Louis and subsequently transported from Paris. The most splendid fragment of the Chamber is the entrance niche, which contains statues of Apollo and Minerva, as well as allegories of Justice and Peace, framing a medallion with a likeness of Stanisław Augustus. The statues were the work of royal court sculptors: the Frenchman Andre Le Brun and the Italian Jacopo Monaldi. Devices of two orders granted by the King – the Order of the White Eagle and the Order of St. Stanisław – are inscribed on two sides of the niche. The Grand Chamber also con-

Royal Castle, Royal Dressing Room and Study; reconstructed in 1971–1984 upon the basis of an unrealised project by Jan Chrystian Kamsetzer from 1792

Royal Castle, Green Room; reconstruction in 1971–1984 referred to Classical forms

Royal Castle, Yellow Room; reconstruction in 1971–1984 referred to Classical forms

Royal Castle, Yellow Room

tains an enormous plafond, painted by Marcello Bacciarelli and presenting the mythological theme of *The Resolving of Chaos*. The fundamental message which the King wished to express through the Chamber's decoration and that of its plafond was belief in the need to " maintain the divine order of the world", envisaged as the duty of every monarch.

In 1779, even while the Grand Chamber was still in the course of being completed, work was initiated on a wing intended for the King's book collection. The Royal Library, built according to projects by Merlini and Kamsetzer, is distinct among all Polish Classical interiors due to its sophisticated architecture in the spirit of the best English accomplishments of the epoch. In 1782, it housed more than 16 000 books, kept in magnificent panelled cases.

The year 1781 marked the beginning of the furnishing of one of the most important Castle chambers – the Knights' Hall, known also as the National Hall. It was devised by King Stanisław Augustus, who wished to create in the Castle a national pantheon commemorating persons who had served the homeland, as well as to recall the most significant moments in the history of Poland. This idea initiated by the King was realised by the architects Merlini and Kamsetzer, the painter Bacciarelli and the sculptors Le Brun and Monaldi. Six large canvases illustrated scenes from the history of Poland and Lithuania, including *The Foundation of the Jagiellonian University in Cracow, The Polish-Lithuanian Union, and The Victory of Jan III Sobieski at Vienna.* Oval portraits and bronze busts depicted famous Poles, personally selected by the monarch: statesmen, commanders, priests and men of letters. The inscription encircling the interior was taken from Book VII of Virgil's *Aeneid*, referring to the deeds of outstanding citizens. The outfitting of the Hall was supplemented by the statues of Fame and Chronos-Saturn. Fame was to proclaim eternal praise for persons distinguished by the King, and Chronos – symbolising the passage of time and the constant revival of life – was to ensure that the features of men renowned in Polish history would be reborn in the young generation. Stanisław Augustus intended to demonstrate the truth that the force and wisdom of a nation, deep faith, and the observation of the principles of justice are the achievement both of monarchs and politicians, clergymen, and men of science and the arts. Within the state apartment, and this was the role played by the Grand Apartment, the Knights' Hall served as the Senators' Antechamber, where, in accordance with the ceremonial of the Polish court, the highest ranking guests of the King: senators and ambassadors, gathered.

The final two interiors created within the Grand Apartment were the Throne Room and the Cabinet of European Monarchs, on which work was commenced in 1783 and completed in 1786. As in the case of the previously described interiors, these too were a collective undertaking of the entire artistic court of Stanisław Augustus, but above all Merlini, Kamsetzer and Jan Bogumił Plersch. The composition of the Throne Room involved the employing of panelling and bronze objects brought over

Royal Castle, Marble Room, eastern and northern wall; 1640–1643, project by Giovanni Battista Gisleni and 1769–1771, project by Jakub Fontana; interior reconstructed in 1971–1984

←

Royal Castle, Marble Room, wall with a portrait of King Stanisław August by Marcello Bacciarelli, about 1769

←

from Paris. In turn, console tables with mosaic tops, four statues of classical statesmen and the fireplaces were purchased in Rome. It follows from the reports by participants at audiences held in the Throne Room that a great impression was made by its lavishness, especially the setting of the royal throne. The entire surface of the throne's backrest and the underneath part of the baldachin were covered with embroidered silver eagles wearing golden crowns, a symbol of the Polish Kingdom. The small, beautifully decorated cabinet adjoining the Throne Room was dedicated to seven monarchs, contemporaries of Stanisław Augustus, whose portraits were featured on walls covered with colourful frescoes. These were Pope Pius VI, Catherine II, Empress of Russia, Joseph II, Emperor of Austria, Gustav III, the King of Sweden, Frederick II, the King of Prussia, Louis XVI, the King of France, and George III, the King of England. The outfitting of the interior was supplemented by a splendid floor made of 13 types of wood, as well as bronze items and a small table of the highest artistic quality with a Sèvres porcelain top. This interior too was given a carefully conceived ideological programme, composed of two intertwining motifs. The first referred to the policies conducted by the portrayed figures, and the second expressed universal contents and ideals, which were to inspire those who wield power. The room served an extremely important function – here, the King received notable guests for private conversations; hence its name – the Conference Room. The royal apartments were supplemented by several apartments intended for the royal family and high state officials (including the apartment of Stanisław Poniatowski, the King's nephew). The last King of Poland left the Castle after his abdication in January 1795.

During the reign of Stanisław Augustus the Castle was a lively theatrical and musical centre. It also played an important role in the political ventures of the Kingdom, and witnessed the birth of such institutions, of foremost rank for the history of the Polish nation, as the Knights' School, the National Theatre and the Commission of National Education. The foremost accomplishment conceived at the Castle was the Constitution of 3 May, passed in 1791.

In 1795–1831, successive partitioners turned the Castle into an official building, and after the suppressing of the November Uprising it became the residence of tsarist governor-generals. Numerous projects made during the Kingdom of Poland pertained to the overall redesigning of the Castle, and in the 1820s buildings standing in front of the western elevation were pulled down, creating Zamkowy Square. As has been mentioned, this task was supervised by the architect Jakub Kubicki, author of an expansive structure known as the Kubicki Arcades, situated at the foot of the Castle escarpment facing the Vistula. The first garden composition was introduced in the area obtained as a result of a change in the course of the Vistula bed.

In the wake of the defeat of the November Uprising, the wall decorations in the Marble Room were taken down and liquidated interiors inc-

Royal Castle, Marble Room, eastern and northern wall with allegories of Justice and Peace

←

Royal Castle, Knights' Hall, statue of Chronos-Saturn, executed by Jacopo Monaldi and André Le Brun, 1781–1786

←

121

Royal Castle, Knights' Hall, statue of Fame-Eternity, executed by Jacopo Monaldi and André Le Brun, 1781–1786

Royal Castle, Knights' Hall, 1781–1786, project by Domenico Merlini and Jan Chrystian Kamsetzer; interior reconstructed in 1971–1984

luded among other rooms, the Senators' Hall. In 1852, the Castle façades received a Late Neoclassical form, based on a project made by Kubicki in 1818–1821.

During the nineteenth century, the Castle and its immediate surrounding were the scenes of great patriotic events. The dethronement of Tsar Nicholas I, proclaimed in the course of the November Uprising of 1831, took place in the Senators' Hall. In the years preceding the outbreak of the January Uprising of 1863 demonstrations, stifled by tsarist troops, were held in Zamkowy Square.

Following the regaining of independence in 1918, the Castle became a representative building; from 1920, it was the residence of the Head of State, and from 1926 – of the President of the Republic of Poland. Discoveries made at that time include the Gothic elevation of *Curia Maior*. In 1927, the removal of Late Neoclassical decoration, dating from the mid-nineteenth century, restored to the Castle façades their appearance from the beginning of the seventeenth century.

At this time, the Castle played an essential role in the mutual permeation of national and state consciousness. The other important political events which took place here included state visits and such spectacles of pomp and ceremony as the presentation to Marshal Józef Piłsudski of the French Medaille Militaire in 1927. On 23 April 1935, the President signed the Constitution, later known as the 1935 Constitution, in the Knights' Hall.

The events of September 1939 posed an immediate threat to the Castle. The siege of Warsaw inflicted extremely grave damage on the city. On 17 September, bombs hit the Grand Hall; the ceiling with the Bacciarelli plafond crashed down, and fire destroyed the Castle roofs. Kazimierz Brokl, the curator of the Castle, perished in the courtyard. Historians of art as well as architects from the Royal Castle and the National Museum in Warsaw salvaged everything they could save from the burnt out ruins. In three weeks, they transferred to the cellars of the National Museum almost 80% of the art works, which fortunately survived wartime conflagration and now constitute the foundation of the outfitting of the Castle interiors.

The onset of Nazi occupation imposed upon the staff of the National Museum in Warsaw the task of preserving the greatest possible number of the original fragments of the Castle furnishing and decoration. Under the supervision of Professor Stanisław Lorentz, director of the Museum, the staff risked their lives under the difficult wartime conditions of 1939–1940 and dismantled the Castle doors, panelling, floors, fireplaces, fragments of stucco and even large parts of murals from the Cabinet of European Monarchs. Haste was necessary since in September 1939 Hitler passed a verdict on the Castle, which was to be demolished, a task for which the Germans made preparations by boring thousands of holes for the purpose of installing explosives. The openings were made in two rows, 75 cms. apart and 1,5 meters above the ground. In the course of two months, several thousand holes were drilled appeared in the Castle walls.

Heavy fighting during the Warsaw Uprising of 1944, and, predominantly, the air attacks, turned the Old Town and its churches into mounds of rubble and ruins. The Castle itself was the battleground of the Old Town Home Army group known as "Róg". The southern wing was seriously damaged, and a fragment of the Castle's western wing was destroyed totally. German sappers used the openings drilled in 1939, in which they now placed explosives, demolishing the Castle walls. The sentence had been carried out – the Castle and the town of Warsaw were supposed to disappear from the Earth's surface for ever.

The Poles never came to terms with this criminal verdict. The Royal Castle was to be rebuilt upon the basis of a decree issued by the Parliament in 1949. Nonetheless, during the following years, all work, even archaeological or of the kind aimed at extracting from the rubble the original fragments of stone decorations, was halted for political reasons. There was, however, a single person who decided to wage a struggle for the Castle's sake – this was Professor Stanisław Lorentz, the then director of the National Museum in Warsaw, who died in 1991. In January 1971, Professor Lorentz secured the passing of a decision to reconstruct the Castle. A suitable project was prepared by Professor Jan Zachwatowicz, and plans for the interiors were set up by a Commission headed by Professor Aleksander Gieysztor. The functions of the general contractor of the reconstruction was entrusted to the State Enterprise Ateliers for the Conservation of Historical Monuments.

The Castle exteriors were ready as early as in July 1974, but the interiors were to take shape gradually over the next ten years, and Warsaw Castle was opened to the public on 31 August 1984. This event was preceded by the establishment of a museum – the Royal Castle in Warsaw, whose newly-nominated director was Professor Aleksander Gieysztor.

The whole reconstruction was financed by Poles at home and abroad. Not a single zloty was taken from the state budge, and a considerable role was played by countries from all over the world – governments, in acts of goodwill to the Polish state, offered several hundred works of art. The accepted general conception of the reconstruction of the Castle assumed the restoration of its state prior to the damage incurred in 1939–1944, and thus the preservation of the former outline of the building and the level of its location, as well as the inclusion of extant elements of walls and decorations into the newly rebuilt ensemble. Such an approach meant that part of the Castle is composed of the original complex of cellars facing the Vistula. The principle employed in rebuilding the interiors imposed a strict recreation of the prewar state, with the application of authentic elements, or upon the basis of iconographic documentation.

The interiors of other apartments: both for royal and state functions, were recreated with utmost precision. The Royal Chapel contains numerous original elements, including the greater part of the six among the eight stucco columns; the same holds true for fragments of domes and walls, or the most magnificent Castle interiors: the Old Audience Room,

Royal Castle, fragment of Throne Room wall

Royal Castle, Throne Room, 1784–1786, project by Domenico Merlini; interior reconstructed in 1971–1984

→

Royal Castle, Throne Room, door leading to the Royal Study, 1784–1786, project by Domenico Merlini; interior reconstructed in 1971–1984

Royal Castle, Throne Room, view of royal throne, 1784–1786; embroidered eagles on the throne backrest reconstructed after 1992

129

←

Royal Castle, fragment of the Cabinet of European Monarchs

*Royal Castle, Cabinet of European
Monarchs, 1783–1786; interior
reconstructed in 1971–1984*

131

Royal Castle, Gallery of Monarchs, new project from 1971–1984, outfitted with, i. a., portraits and statues depicting European monarchs from the sixteenth to the eighteenth centuries

Royal Castle, Council Chamber, new project from 1971–1984, using original decoration elements from the 1770s and 1780s

Royal Castle, Oval Gallery, outfitted with, i. a. Brussels tapestries from the mid-sixteenth century, new project from 1971–1984

Royal Castle, Senators' Hall, about 1740; reconstructed in 1971–1984 upon the basis of a project by Zachariasz Longelune from 1721–1722

Royal Castle, Senators' Hall, royal throne

Royal Castle, Concert Hall (Old Chapel),
1744–1746, project probably
by Zachariasz Longelune; interior
reconstructed in 1971–1984

←

the King's Bedroom, the Grand Hall, the Knights' Hall, the Throne Room, and the Cabinet of European Monarchs, all of which were rebuilt in accordance with their pre-1939 appearance. Hundreds of original elements were incorporated into the walls. By way of example, in the Old Audience Room, they included the imperial eagles over the mirrors, in the King's Bedroom – more than 50% of the yew panelling, in the Throne Room – hundreds of original fragments of the panelling and stucco work, and in the Cabinet of European Monarchs – original fragments of the murals, a truly unique phenomenon. Unfortunately, it proved impossible to save the decorative ceilings in the Old Audience Room and the Grand Hall; during the most recent reconstruction, they were recreated upon the basis of descriptions and original sketches from the period. Part of the outfitting of the royal chambers and rooms survived, including the above mentioned canvases by Bernardo Bellotto from the Canaletto Room, paintings by Bacciarelli from the Old Audience Room, the Bedroom and the Knights' Hall, sculptures from the Grand Hall and the Throne Room as well as furniture, bronze objects and a number of fireplaces. An exception was the royal bed, lost already in the nineteenth century, as well as the decoration of the royal throne. The latter was recreated upon the basis of old drawings and descriptions, while reconstruction of the royal throne's decoration, including the silver embroidered eagles, was possible thanks to the discovery of the only extant eagle (in 1991).

In the area of the Marble Room, the Senators' Hall and the Deputies' Chamber on the first storey the situation was different, since these interiors had simply ceased to exist as early as in the first half of the nineteenth century, and thus could be reconstructed thanks only to reliable drawings preserved in Polish and foreign archives. It must be added that in the Marble Room use was made of original elements, such as sculptures, fragments of marble and doors as well as original furnishings – all the portraits of the Polish kings and wall candlesticks.

Despite the fact that the Royal Castle contains relics from earlier epochs, it remains, generally speaking, an Early Baroque work. This was the time of the origin of the most characteristic features of the building. Walking along Krakowskie Przedmieście towards Zamkowy Square our attention is drawn by the Castle's severe monumental exterior form, with the vivid accents of its towers and the sophisticated simplicity in the decorations of its stone portals, corners and window frames. The light-coloured masonry contrasts with the red plaster of the façades; the high shingle roof and the elegantly outlined tower finials form charming fragments of the Old Town landscape. This effect becomes even more marked when we admire the panorama of Warsaw from the Vistula, with the Late Baroque façade, brimming with *chiaroscuro* effects and embellished with refined sculpted decorations. Once we enter the vast Courtyard, where the inner elevation reflects the centuries-long history of the building, we observe the entire history of the Castle. The Gothic façade of the former *Curia Maior* brings to mind the dukes of Mazovia, the oldest owners of the

Royal Castle, New Deputies' Chamber, end of seventeenth century; reconstructed in 1971–1984 upon the basis of an inventory of the Chamber from about 1740

Royal Castle, Four Seasons' Gallery, new project from 1971–1984; tapestries woven by Françoise Glaize

Royal Castle, Social Life Room in the apartment of Prince Stanisław Poniatowski, panelling from about the mid-eighteenth century

Royal Castle, Antechamber in the apartment of Prince Stanisław Poniatowski, panelling from about the mid-eighteenth century

Castle, the Early Baroque western elevation and the decoration of the Władysław Tower recall monarchs from the Vasa dynasty, and the façade of the northern wing – rulers from the Wettin dynasty, while the façade of the southern wing reminds us that this part was rebuilt upon the initiative of the last Polish monarch.

A careful observation of the façade's stonework decoration demonstrates how many of its fragments were salvaged from the rubble of the demolished Castle and meticulously installed into the gate portals, window frames and other fragments. It must be borne in mind that not even thirty years ago the Royal Castle did not exist in its spatial structure, but there were hundreds of thousands of its original fragments and hundreds of original works of art, once belonging to its interior. All were reinstated, and are decisive for the historical character of the former royal residence.

At present, the Royal Castle is a museum open to the public and the site of important state ceremonies. The rich interiors depict the history and tradition of the Polish nation and state. A combination of tradition and contemporaneity enables it to become a place for shaping the historical and aesthetic sensitivity of the Poles.

The Royal Castle is known to millions, both visitors and those who saw its interiors in numerous television broadcasts of state ceremonies and cultural and social meetings.

Ceremonies held in the Castle chambers are organised by supreme state offices – the Sejm and the Senate as well as the Chancellery of the President. Many such events already possess a certain tradition of their own. The most important include the presentation of awards for outstanding scientific, cultural and economic accomplishments. The Castle also plays host to prominent international conferences, such as those organised by the Council of Europe or the European Union.

Outstanding visitors have included: Pope John Paul II (twice), H. R. M. Queen Elizabeth II of the United Kingdom, King Charles XVI Gustav of Sweden, King Juan Carlos of Spain, Queen Margaret II of Denmark, Queen Beatrice of the Netherlands, King Albert of Belgium, Boris Yeltsin, President of Russia, George Bush, President of the United States (twice), Bill Clinton, President of the United States, François Mitterand, ex-President of France, Helmut Kohl, former Chancellor of Germany, and many others.

Every year, about 100 000 children and young people attend specially organised museum lessons held at the Castle. Other events include art and historical exhibitions, theatre spectacles and lecture series. The Concert Hall and the Grand Hall feature concerts, such as those performed as part of the annual Mozart Festival and the Festival of Old Music.

The Castle area facing the Vistula is undergoing gradual changes. Work is being conducted on a reconstruction of the Castle gardens, and thorough conservation is being carried out in the so-called Kubicki Arcades at the foot of the escarpment, one of the few fragments of the Castle to have escaped destruction during the second world war.

Royal Castle, Royal Library, 1779–1782, project by Domenico Merlini and Jan Chrystian Kamsetzer

Royal Castle, Former Deputies' Vestibule, 1569–1572 and 1600–1604; interior reconstructed in 1971–1984

*Royal Castle, Grand Hall, 1777–1781,
project by Domenico Merlini
and Jan Chrystian Kamsetzer,
interior reconstructed in 1971–1984*

*Royal Castle Ducal Cellar, first
quarter of the fifteenth century*

*Royal Castle, Small Chapel
Sanctuary, fragment of the dome*

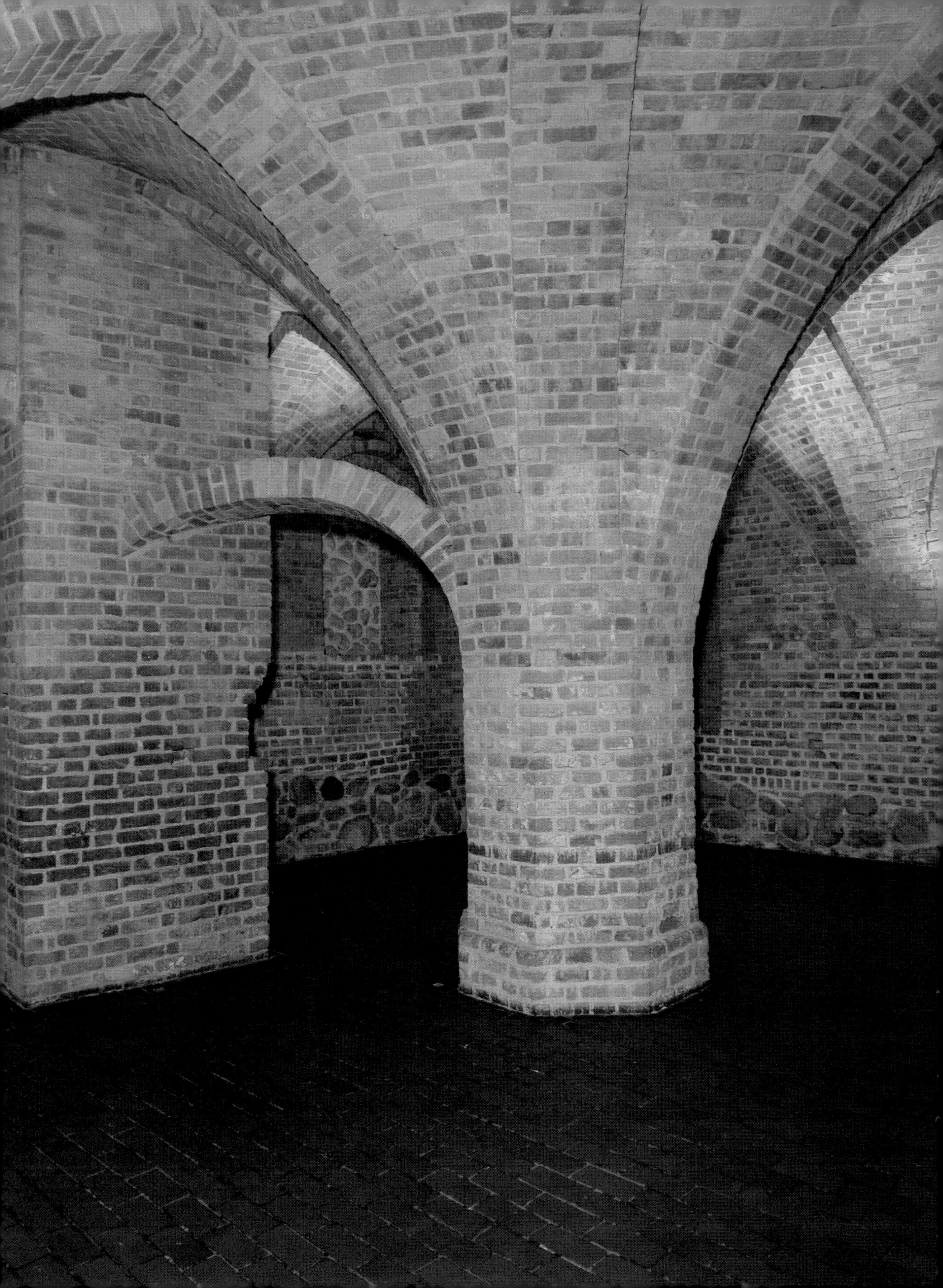

The beginnings of the historical centre of Warsaw coincide with the inclusion of Mazovia into the Polish Crown in 1526. A consecutive essential date was the year 1770, when Warsaw was encircled by the earthworks raised upon the initiative of Stanisław Lubomirski, the Grand Crown Marshal. For almost 150 years, they comprised the boundary of the entire urban organism, and it was precisely within their range that the historical centre developed. Not until the inter-war period were those limits crossed during the dynamic emergence of such districts as Żoliborz, Ochota, Mokotów or Saska Kępa.

The basic town-planning structure of the central districts was discussed in the chapter on the history of Warsaw; here, we shall present more details concerning spatial and architectural development.

Within the extensive area of the town centre, the centre assumed different shapes in relation to different periods. For quite a long time, until the beginning of the nineteenth century, the centre consisted of the region adjoining the Royal Castle, i. e. the square in front of Krakowska Gate, together with the Przedmiejski (Suburban) or Bernardyński (Bernardine) Market Square; the Column of Zygmunt III, situated here, became the most vivid landmark. During the Kingdom of Poland, the proper centre came into being in Krakowskie Przedmieście and several squares delineated at the time (Bankowy, Teatralny); in the later decades of the nineteenth century, it shifted into the region of Marszałkowska Street and its side streets. A distinct central district did not emerge after the second world war, despite attempts made during the 1950s at localising it in the environs of the Palace of Culture and Science or the Marszałkowska Residential District. Two centuries passed before the area of the Royal Castle and the Old Town were restored to their rank of a cultural centre, although a closely defined banking-commercial centre, so characteristic for great metropolises, is still missing. It is from this very viewpoint that the Warsaw town planners face the task of coordinating the investment tide of the past few years.

Let us return to the city centre's origins. Already in the fourteenth century a wide square known as the Bernardyński (later: Przedmiejski) Market Square was created in front of the southern town gate (Krakowska), more or less on the spot where the Zygmunt Column stands today. Along its western side there appeared a compact line of burgher houses, and ducal gardens stretched along the eastern side. Some of them, situated between present-day Bednarska Street and the Carmelite church as well as on both sides of today's Trębacka Street, were granted by Duke Janusz the Older to the deans and the collegiate church, creating an area known as Dziekania (1402). Another part of the gardens was planned by Duchess Anna Holszańska in 1454 as an area for the construction of a Bernardine monastery and church (today: St. Anne's), while the remaining part, reaching as far as the road in the gorge of the Kamionka stream, was offered to the town, burghers, clergymen and courtiers. In 1450–1526, the ducal landed estate, on both sides of present-day Krakowskie Przedmieście, up to a fork in the direction of Solec and Jazdów, became the property of burghers and the

Fragment of the statue of Prince Józef Poniatowski in Krakowskie Przedmieście Street; new cast from 1826–1832, executed by Bertel Thorvaldsen

145

Painting depicting the Madonna and Child in the church gable of St. Anne (facing the escarpment)

Complex of eighteenth-century houses in Krakowskie Przedmieście Street, between Zamkowy Square and Miodowa Street; in the foreground, the shaft of the old Column of King Zygmunt III

Bernardine (academic) church of St. Anne in Krakowskie Przedmieście Street, façade from 1786–1788, acc. to a project by Chrystian Piotr Aigner and Stanisław Kostka Potocki

St. Anne church in Krakowskie Przedmieście Street, presbytery from the second half of the fifteenth century

146

Fragment of the plinth of the Adam Mickiewicz statue in Krakowskie Przedmieście Street

Civic Club in Krakowskie Przedmieście Street, 1860–1861, project by Edward Cichocki; reconstructed after wartime damage, 1948–1950

Missionaries and vicars of the collegiate church of St. John. A chapel of the Holy Cross was erected by this road, and a section of the latter, leading from Przedmiejski Market Square, became known as the ku św. Krzyżowi (to the Holy Cross) Route.

The essential spatial development of Warsaw began when Mazovia became part of the Polish Crown and Warsaw was granted the status of a residential town. As has been mentioned, the redesigning and expansion of Warsaw Castle served as the most distinct symbol of this new status – its monumental exterior outline became the foremost landmark in the spatial composition of the town as a whole.

This was the period of a wider-scale emergence of the aforementioned areas within the town; typical for Warsaw, they were known as jurisdictions (*jurydki*). Alongside the Church *jurydyki* – Dziekania, Świętojerska and Bernardine, which came into being outside the town walls already in the Middle Ages, the rights of a jurisdiction were enjoyed by monastic property, such as Nowolipie (property of the Bridgetin nuns) or Nowogrodzka (property of the Paulite monks). Newly created jurisdictions included the Zadzikowska (Church property, town rights from 1638), which occupied the area between Podwale and Miodowa streets, along both sides of Kapitulna Street; below the escarpment, on the south side of today's Tamka Street, Queen Ludwika Maria founded an ecclesiastical jurisdiction (town rights in 1652), known as Tamka, for the Sisters of Mercy who had been brought over from France and built the extant church of St. Kazimierz and a co-

Building of the Warsaw Charity Society in Krakowskie Przedmieście Street, 1819, project by Antonio Corazzi; rebuilt after wartime devastation, 1949–1960

Krakowskie Przedmieście Street at the corner of Trębacka and Kozia streets; to the left, the building of the Saxon Post from the end of the eighteenth century.

Inn (known as Dziekanka) in Krakowskie Przedmieście Street, 1770–1784

Statue of Adam Mickiewicz in Krakowskie Przedmieście Street, 1898, executed by Cyprian Godebski

The Presidential (Koniecpolski, Radziwiłł, Governor) Palace in Krakowskie Przedmieście Street, 1643, redesigned in 1818–1819 acc. to a project by Chrystian Piotr Aigner

Statue of Prince Józef Poniatowski in Krakowskie Przedmieście Street, 1826–1832, executed by Bertel Thorvaldsen; new cast

nvent, which stand to this day. The brothers Bogusław and Jan Leszczyński founded the Leszno jurisdiction (town rights in 1648) on a narrow strip of cultivated land purchased from the Warsaw burghers, between present-day General Anders Street and Żelazna Street. The main street of this regularly planned jurisdiction was today's Leszno Street.

The Grzybów jurisdiction (town rights in 1650) was established by Jan Grzybowski, the starosta of Warsaw, on part of the terrains belonging to the office of the Warsaw (*starostwo*), which encompassed an area outlined by the following present-day streets: Swiętokrzyska (to the south), Marszałkowska and Graniczna (to the east), Towarowa (to the west) and Chłodna (to the north). The road which was to link the landed estate of the *starosta* and Grzybów became the core of the future Królewska Street.

The town bulwarks, erected in 1621–1624, embraced the Old and the New Towns and the majority of jurisdictions, landed estates, palaces and manors. The northern boundary of this area was today's Wójtowska Street, the western – Bankowy Square, and the southern – Karowa Street. The suburbs, protected by the bulwarks, were developed intensively and put in order. In 1643, the area in front of Krakowska Gate was prepared for the erecting of the Column of Zygmunt III – in this way creating a representative town square, closely associated with the functioning of the royal residence.

In the ensuing years, the division of suburban land advanced beyond the bulwarks and followed, on the whole, routes leading to the city. Wooden buildings were erected along the future Nowy Swiat Street and its side stre-

Carmelite church of the Assumption of the Holy Virgin Mary and St. Joseph the Bridegroom in Krakowskie Przedmieście Street, 1661–1672 and 1680–1682, façade 1761–1783, acc. to a project by Efraim Schroeger

151

150. *"Victoria" Hotel in Królewska Street, built in 1974–1976 acc. to a project by A. W. Dzierżawski, D. Fraser, K. Hultin, S. Kaim, Z. Pawelski and L. Sołonowicz*

The Potocki Palace in Krakowskie Przedmieście Street, erected in 1760–1766; reconstructed after wartime damage, 1948–1950

"Bristol" Hotel in Krakowskie Przedmieście Street, 1899–1901, project by Władysław Marconi

Emblem of Warsaw University in the finial of the gate grating seen from Krakowskie Przedmieście Street

The Tyszkiewicz-Potocki Palace in Krakowskie Przedmieście Street, 1785–1792, project by Stanisław Zawadzki and Jan Chrystian Kamsetzer; rebuilt after wartime devastation, 1948–1951

Gate of Warsaw University, built in 1909–1910 acc. to a project by Stefan Szyller

Kazimierzowski Palace (offices of the Rector of Warsaw University), original building from 1634, redesigned upon numerous occasions; façade facing the courtyard rebuilt after wartime damages in Classical forms, 1946–1954

→

So-called Seminary Building of Warsaw University, 1815–1816, project by Jakub Kubicki

→

The Staszic Palace at the end of Krakowskie Przedmieście Street, 1820–1823, project by Antonio Corazzi; rebuilt after wartime damage, 1946–1951

ets: Swiętokrzyska and Chmielna. In the north, land division reached the region of today's Żoliborz, and in the west – present-day Żelazna Street. Particularly lively development appeared to the south of the town, near the ku św. Krzyżowi Route (today: Krakowskie Przedmieście) – the church-monastic complexes of the Carmelites, brought to Poland in 1637, the Missionaries (1651; today, the church of the Holy Cross), and the Visitant nuns (1654). Here, there appeared the royal palace of Władysław IV – the so-called *villa regia*, the palaces of Adam Kazanowski, Stanisław Koniecpolski, Jerzy Ossoliński and Mikołaj Daniłowicz, and the manors of the Radziwiłł, Mokronowski, Tarło and Gembicki families. The western part of the town became the site of newly erected church-monastic complexes: the Reformed Franciscans (Senatorska Street), brought to Poland in 1623, the Piarists (Długa Street), brought in 1642, and the Bridgetin nuns (Długa Street; the ensemble was pulled down in the nineteenth century), who arrived in 1628.

Gradually, the appearance of the suburbs of Warsaw also changed, and a new Baroque form prevailed in the town landscape. An example of the adoption of the modern palace structure, which originated in the Italian villa and the French chateau, was the royal *villa regia*, i. e. the later Kazimierzowski Palace, raised on the high Warsaw escarpment. This was a singular site, where, starting with the sixteenth century, dozens of residences were built by utilising the natural assets of the terrain. Palaces and manors were erected at the top of the escarpment, and their gardens descended towards the Vistula in terraces.

The Czapski Palace in Krakowskie Przedmieście Street, original from 1680–1705, later redesigned, façade from 1752–1765; reconstructed after wartime devastation, 1948–1951

(Former Missionary) church of the Finding of the Holy Cross in Krakowskie Przedmieście Street, built in 1679–1696 acc. to a project by Józef Szymon Bellotti, façade from 1725–1737 acc. to a project by Józef Fontana; reconstructed after wartime damage, 1945–1953

Figure of Christ in front of the church of the Holy Cross in Krakowskie Przedmieście Street, 1858, executed by Andrzej Pruszyński

View of houses in the Mariensztat residential estate, built in 1948–1949 acc. to a project by Zygmunt Stępiński

Palace of the Bishops of Cracow in Miodowa Street; reconstruction after wartime devastation referred to Late Baroque forms, 1948–1951

The Primate's Palace, original from the end of the seventeenth century, redesigned in 1777–1783 acc. to a project by Efraim Schroeger; rebuilt after wartime damage, 1949–1952

Statue of Mikołaj Kopernik in front of the Staszic Palace, 1830, executed by Bertel Thorvaldsen

Basilian church of the Assumption of the Holy Virgin Mary in Miodowa Street, 1782–1784, project by Domenico Merlini; reconstructed after wartime devastation, 1946–1949

The Raczyński Palace in Długa Street, original building from 1702–1704, redesigned in 1786 acc. to a project by Jan Chrystian Kamsetzer; rebuilt after wartime damage, 1948–1950

Capuchin church of the Transfiguration of the Lord in Miodowa Street,
1683–1692, project by Tylman of Gameren and Augustyn Locci

The Radziwiłł (Pac) Palace gate in Miodowa Street, 1681–1697,
project by Tylman of Gameren; palace redesigned in 1824–1828

The aftermath of the Swedish "deluge" led to the birth of four jurisdictions: the Nowoświecka jurisdiction (Church property, 1659) was administratively linked with the Zadzikowska and the Dziekańska, and encompassed several lots along both sides of Nowy Swiat, to the south of Warecka and Ordynacka streets. To the west, the fields of this jurisdiction stretched in a narrow strip, limited by the later Sienna and Złota streets. The Aleksandryjska jurisdiction (magnate property, 1670) was founded by Aleksander Zasławski on land along the northern side of Tamka Street, between Aleksander, Oboźna and Dobra streets, and included the later Leszczyńska, Drewniana and Zajęcza streets. Part of the land belonging to the Warsaw *starostwo* contained the Wielopole jurisdiction (magnate property, 1693), established by Maria Anna de la Grange d'Arquien, widow of Jan Wielopolski, the Crown Chancellor. To the south and the west, this so-called townlet adjoined Grzybów; to the north, its boundary was Elektoralna Street, and to the east – the future Żabia and Graniczna streets. Similarly to the earlier Leszno, Wielopole was established in accordance with a carefully devised street plan, which envisaged the satisfying of an independent small town's needs, and included, among other features, a market square and a town hall. The fourth jurisdiction was Bożydar (magnate property, 1702), established in the environs of Nowy Swiat by Józef Szwarcenberg-Czerny, castellan of Sącz. This jurisdiction included an area on both sides of Nowy Swiat Street – Smolna, Książęca, Bracka and Chmielna streets.

Land reserves for eventual division into building lots consisted of fields comprising the landed estate of the office of the Warsaw *starosta*. They included vast territories in almost the very centre of the Warsaw suburbs, to a great extent already divided. As early as 1669, this was the site of the church of the Knights Hospitallers of St. John (in the later Saxon Garden, today: Królewska Street) and about 17 noble manors, including the earlier mentioned Morsztyn Palace.

The several churches built at this time, which subsequently became important elements in the urban panorama, include: the Piarist church in Długa Street (1678–1681), the Franciscan church in Zakroczymska Street (1680–1698), the Reformed Franciscan church in Senatorska Street (1671–1678), the Missionary church in Krakowskie Przedmieście (1679–1696), the Carmelite church in Leszno (construction inaugurated in 1683) and the Capuchin church in Miodowa Street, built in 1683–1692; the latter object provided a pattern emulated by authors of numerous churches throughout the country.

The important place held by Warsaw in the history of Polish architecture at the end of the seventeenth century was attained, to a large degree, thanks to the extraordinary talent of the architect Tylman of Gameren. Churches and palaces erected according to his projects left an extremely vivid imprint on the town's appearance. The church of the Sisters of the Blessed Sacrament (1688–1692) and the adjoining Kotowski Palace (1683–1688) endowed the New Town Market Square with the character of a representative municipal square. The artistically outstanding palace of Jan Dobrogost Krasiński (1689–1694) comprised the centre of one of the most impressive urban palace complexes on a European scale. The Gniński Palace (1681–1685) in Tamka Street, built as part of an originally much wider scheme, became an essential feature of the Warsaw panorama, as seen from the Vistula. The Radziwiłł Palace in Miodowa Street (1673–1697), a celebrated realisation by Tylman of Gameren, to a large measure designated the scale of Warsaw architecture. A foremost town investment, raised according to another design by Tylman, was the previously mentioned Marywil (today: the region of Teatralny Square). Erected in 1682–1696 by Queen Maria Kazimiera, it contained several score shops, commodity storehouses, a tavern, residential apartments, spectacle halls, a chapel and a monastery.

The further development of central Warsaw was affected by new town-planning premises from the reign of Augustus II and Augustus III, especially the so-called Saxon Axis and Kalwaryjska Route.

The main composition axis, of Saxon origin, ran from Krakowskie Przedmieście, crossing Saski (Saxon) Square (today: the Tomb of the Unknown Soldier) and further, to the west, across the Saski (Saxon) Garden, between pavilions of the Crown Horse Guards barracks (Chłodna Street). The terrain of the premise was embraced by a radial pattern of approach avenues (including Królewska Street), whose eastern focus point was the Palace courtyard, and the western one – the newly created square in the area between today's Lubomirski Palace and first of the two Mirów mar-

162

Statue of Cardinal Stefan Wyszyński, Primate of Poland, in front of the Visitant church, 1986, executed by Andrzej Renes

---→

STEFAN
KARDYNAŁ
WYSZYŃSKI
PRYMAS POLSKI

ket halls. The impressive scale of the Saxon Axis brutally cut the town in two, and considerably restricted its proper development. The second town-planning premise was associated with the residence in Ujazdów, where a large-scale complex was planned. Its centre was to consist of Ujazdów Castle, expanded into a church and a monastery, and the main town-planning element was to be Kalwaryjska Route. Created in 1724–1731 (today: Ujazdowskie Avenue) as a vista and communication link between Ujazdów and the Old Town, it soon turned into one of the most important arteries of the capital, which has not lost its significance to this very day. An element of the Ujazdów urban layout, which illustrates the scale of town-planning projects under the Saxon kings, is the length of the royal canal, known as Piaseczyński and delineated along the Castle axis in 1720–1731.

The range of activity pursued by the two Saxon monarchs included only a single architectural design which became a permanent part of the urban landscape and proved to possess consequences for the further history of Polish architecture. This was the corpus of Warsaw Castle, facing the Vistula and erected in 1741–1746.

Magnates continued to create town jurisdictions; three new ones originated during this period. The Ordynacka jurisdiction, established by Michał Zamoyski, was granted town rights in 1739 and encompassed terrains to the east of Nowy Swiat Street. The Mariensztat jurisdiction, founded in 1762 by Eustachy and Maria (born Kątska) Potocki at the foot of the escarpment to the south of the Royal Castle incroporated seven streets, together with a market square and a town hall, and constituted an important trade-crafts centre.

In contrast to secular architecture, a much more distinct imprint upon the image of the town was left by sacral architecture. Effective façades were given to, among others, churches in Krakowskie Przedmieście: the Visitant church (1728), the Holy Cross (completed in 1756) and the non-extant church of the Observant Dominicans (1727–1731 and after 1760), which stood near the site of today's Staszic Palace.

To a significant extent, the image of the City was shaped by the town-planning and architectural undertakings of King Stanisław Augustus and his courtiers. This holds true predominantly for two earlier described town-planning ventures, one of them being a design for the southern part of the Warsaw whose main accents were stellar squares: today's Zbawiciel Square, Na Rozdrożu Square, the square in front of the present-day Polytechnic, and Unia Lubelska Square. The second undertaking was the erection of the so-called Lubomirski bulwarks, encircling the town (1770).

Apart from those most important initiatives, Stanisław Augustus was also responsible for more modest ones, just as essential for supplementing the urban fabric of the city centre. During the early years of his reign, the King showed interest in Powiśle. In 1768, he founded the Stanisławowo jurisdiction, named after him, on land purchased back from the Sułkowski family in 1765 and embracing an area below Kazimierzowski Palace and present-

The Krasiński Palace (of the Republic) in Krasiński Square, erected in 1677–1697 acc. to a project by Tylman of Gameren; rebuilt after wartime damage, 1948–1961

Post-Piarist church of the Holy Virgin Mary Queen of the Crown of Poland (today: Cathedral of the Armed Forces) in Długa Street, 1660–1681, completed prior to 1712; reconstructed after wartime devastation, 1946–1960

Visitant church of the Custody of St. Joseph in Krakowskie Przedmieście Street, built in 1772–1733 and 1754–1763 acc. to a project by Karol Bay and Efraim Schroeger

Supreme Court in Krasiński Square, erected in 1996–1999 acc. to a project by M. Budzyński and Z. Badowski. In the foreground, the monument of the Heroes of the Warsaw Uprising, 1989, executed by W. Kućma

Arsenal in Długa Street; reconstruction in 1949–1950 referred to forms of the original building from 1638–1643 and its later numerous redesigning

The Maria Radziwiłłowa Palace in Długa Street; rekonstruction in 1951–1957 after wartime damage referred to pre-1939 forms of the Palace

Palace of the Government Revenue and Treasury Commission in Bankowy Square, erected in 1823–1825 acc. to a project by Antonio Corazzi; rebuilt after wartime damage, 1949–1954

day Radna, Wiślana, Lipowa, Browarna and Leszczyńska streets. The gradually developed side streets of Marszałkowska Street were laid out along former fields.

In order to enlarge the Łazienki Park and put its environs into order, the King ordered the removal of the village of Ujazdów from present-day Ujazdowski Park; the same fate was to befall fields in the upper Łazienki terraces and the later Botanical Gardens. The inhabitants of the liquidated homes were transferred to a newly erected settlement, known as Nowa Wieś (the region of today's Nowowiejska Street), designed in accordance with the principles of Enlightenment town planning. The Koszyki royal landed estate was situated at the crossing of present-day Koszykowa, Poznańska and Lwowska streets.

Starting with the 1770s, the division of land into lots affected also newly created streets located to the west of New Warsaw: Stawki, Niska, Miła,

Muranowska, Gęsia, Pawia and Dzielna, and their side streets: Dzika and Smocza.

The extensive division of land also took place in the south-western part of town. Here, the dominant spatial accent was the Saxon layout and two large jurisdictions: Grzybów and Leszno. At the beginning of the 1760s, their houses were scattered and reached as far as the region of present-day Żelazna Street. During the reign of Stanisław Augustus, a number of streets: Grzybowska, Krochmalna, Chłodna, Elektoralna, Ogrodowa, Nowolipie, Żytnia and Nowolipki were extended to the line of the Lubomirski bulwarks. Their side streets: Ciepła, Waliców, Solna, Żelazna and Wronia were delineated.

During the reign of Stanisław Augustus, the city's Baroque appearance was disguised by the introduction of Neoclassical buildings. Nevertheless, this process did not alter the appearance of Warsaw entirely. The most cha-

169

"Blue" – "Silver" skyscraper in Bankowy Square, built in 1976–1992 acc. to a project by Andrzej Skopiński and Jolanta Lipińska

Building of the Jewish Historical Institute in Tłomackie Street, erected in 1928–1936 acc. to a project by Edward Z. Eber

Statue of Stefan Starzyński, President of Warsaw, in Bankowy Square, 1993, executed by Andrzej Renes

171

Reformed Franciscan church of St. Anthony of Padua in Senatorska Street, erected in 1671–1681; rebuilt after wartime damage, 1946–1956

The Franciszek Dembiński Palace at the corner of Senatorska and Daniłowiczowska streets; reconstruction in 1950 referred to forms of early Classical architecture

Façade of Wielki Theatre in Teatralny Square, built in 1825–1833 acc. to a project by Antonio Corazzi

172

racteristic objects in the panorama of the town were still the palaces erected by Tylman of Gameren and lofty, Baroque church towers. More essential changes occurred in the appearance of the representative streets. In Krakowskie Przedmieście, Neoclassical façades were added to the Carmelite (1761–1762) and Bernardine churches (1786–1788). The impressive Roessler and Hurtig house was built opposite the latter church (1784), and the severe exterior form of the Tyszkiewicz palace (1785–1792) became a distinct landmark next to the Visitant church. The Jabłonowski Palace (the later Town Hall, 1768–1778, at present reconstructed) and the elegant residence of Piotr Blank were erected in Senatorska Street (1762–1764). Neoclassical forms were given to the redesigned seat of the Primate, situated in the same street (1777–1783). Baroque buildings along Miodowa Street now included

The Zaluski Library (the "Under the Kings" building) in Hipoteczna Street, 1740–1747; reconstructed after wartime damage, 1960–1962

Statue of Marshal Józef Piłsudski in Piłsudski Square, 1995, executed by Tadeusz Łodziana

Saski (Saxon) Garden. Fountain next to the Grave of the Unknown Soldier, 1855, project by Henryk Marconi

Fragment of Saski Palace. Columnade framing the Grave of the Unknown Soldier

Building of the Society for the Promotion of the Fine Arts in Małachowski Square, erected in 1898–1900 and 1903 acc. to a project by Stefan Szyller

The Schenkler house in Dąbrowski Square, built in 1881–1883 acc. to a project by Witold Lanci

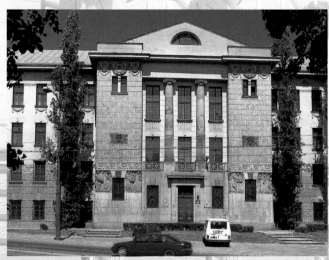

The Records Office building in Solidarności Avenue, erected in 1903 acc. to a project by Henryk Julian Gay and Mikołaj Możdżeński

Evangelical church in Małachowski Square, built in 1777–1781 acc. to a project by Szymon Bogumił Zug

The Przebendowski (Radziwiłł) Palace in Solidarności Avenue, built in 1727–1728; reconstructed after wartime devastation, 1948–1949

Monument of the Heroes of Warsaw, known as the Warsaw Nike, in Solidarności Avenue, 1964, executed by Marian Konieczny

the characteristic frontage of the Tepper house (1774; its ruins were demolished after 1945 in connection with the building of the W–Z Route). Długa Street was also granted a Neoclassical appearance: from the side of Freta Street it now displayed the Neoclassical Raczyński Palace(1786–1787), and at the other end of the street – the palace of Piotr Fergusson Tepper, known as "Under the Four Winds" (end of the 1760s). One of the more powerful accents in the skyline was the dome of the austere, monumental Evangelical church built by Szymon Bogumił Zug in today's Małachowski Square (1777–1781). Another strongly distinguishable edifice was the non-extant palace of Janusz and Karolina Sanguszko (about 1780), erected on the escarpment, in the region of Aleksandria Street. In the western part of the town, a reserved Neoclassical form characterised the large commercial-hotel complex (so-called Tłomackie), erected for Karol Schultz after 1783; its only surviving element is the architectonic setting of a well, known as Gruba Kaśka.

During the long era of Poland's partition, a period which exerted special impact on the appearance of the town and especially the city centre, was that of the Kingdom of Poland (1815–1830). Alongside the tens of public utility buildings, which I mentioned while discussing the history of the capital, the number of new houses erected in Warsaw, and granting it the image of a true metropolis, totalled 419. These were brick edifices, with two or three floors, usually of five or seven bays and modestly embellished. Their appearance was to a considerable degree defined by the construction regulations in force, which determined strictly the course of confirming a project, the type of building material, the manner of placing a house along the line of a given street, the number of storeys, roof height, and even the colour of the plaster.

Although Warsaw houses constituted the main theme of the town's construction in 1815–1830, the architecture of the Kingdom of Poland owed its exceptional position to larger public utility buildings, and it is primarily they which are associated with the accomplishments of the epoch. More than forty such buildings were either raised or older edifices, completely redesigned. On the other hand, no new private residences, so characteristic for Warsaw during the preceding two centuries, were erected. The role of the patron was assumed by the state authorities and the Warsaw middle class.

The most impressive architectural realisations of the 1815–1830 period were situated along the so-called royal route, leading from Zamkowy Square to the Belvedere Palace (Belweder), and along Senatorska Street to Bankowy Square. A new architectural setting was given to the Bernardine bell tower in Krakowskie Przedmieście, and the slightly receding monastery was now preceded by an architectural structure with an arcade frontal elevation, envisaged as the main town guardhouse. Together with the façade of St. Anne's church, dating from the 1780s, the new buildings constituted an impressive complex, generally regarded as one of the more magnificent in the capital.

In 1818–1819, the former Baroque Koniecpolski (Radziwiłł) Palace in Krakowskie Przedmieście was adapted for a governor's residence (today:

Monument of the Heroes of the Ghetto in Zamenhof Street, 1948, executed by Natan Rappaport (sculpture) and Leon Marek Suzin (architecture)

178

NARÓD ŻYDOWSKI
SWYM BOJOWNIKOM
I MĘCZENNIKOM

דאָס יידישע פֿאָלק
זײַנע קעמפֿער
און מאַרטירער

עם ישראל
ללוחמיו ולקדושיו

Wall – Monument of Suffering and Death (Umschlagplatz) in Stawki Street, 1988, executed by Hanna Schmalenberg and Władysław Klamerus

Pawiak – Martyrdom Mausoleum in Dzielna Street, 1965–1966, project by Romuald Gutt, Mieczysław Mołdawa and Alina Scholtzówna (plants)

the Presidential Palace). Warsaw University, situated on the same side of the street, was given a new seat – the former residence of King Jan Kazimierz. In 1829–1825, a Late Baroque church of the Observant Dominicans (to 1818) at the end of Krakowskie Przedmieście was demolished to make way for an imposing building to house the Society of the Friends of Sciences, which in 1830 became the backdrop for a statue of Nicolaus Copernicus, executed by the outstanding Danish sculptor Bertel Thorvaldsen. The most elegant street of the capital was Nowy Swiat, which reached the large Trzech Krzyży Square, an historically important junction of routes leading from the Old Town to Solec, Ujazdów, Rakowiec and Grzybów. Regulated already during the reign of Stanisław Augustus, this square remained unexpanded until the time of the Kingdom of Poland, when it received significant architectonic accents, the most important being a rotunda church, built by Chrystian Piotr Aigner in 1818–1825. The newly widened section of Ujazdowskie Avenue between Na Rozdrożu Square and Piękna Street created a square known as Ujazdowski. At the end of the Avenue, at the spot where it became Belwederska Street, there now stood the Belvedere, which owes its present-day architectonic form to the thorough redesigning performed by Jakub Kubicki in 1818–1822.

The architecture of the Kingdom of Poland left a particular imprint on the area of Teatralny Square, Senatorska Street and Bankowy Square. In

The Mostowski Palace (Government Commission for Internal Affairs and Religion), redesigned upon the basis of an earlier building from 1823 acc. to a project by Antonio Corazzi

The Lubomirski Palace in Żelaznej Bramy Square, redesigned upon the basis of an earlier building from 1791–1793 acc. to a project by Jakub Hempel; reconstructed after wartime damage, 1948–1951

1823–1828, Antonio Corazzi created the prime accomplishments in his career, and, simultaneously, one of the most interesting parts of the capital, i. e. a complex of government buildings in Bankowy Square. Together, they comprise an over 200 metre-long monumental ensemble in a square which widened at the exit of Senatorska and Elektoralna streets, and grew narrower towards the north.

In 1825, Corazzi started work on a building whose scale and impetus is comparable with the greatest realisations in Europe at the time. This was the Wielki (Grand) Theatre, erected in 1825–1833 in Teatralny Square. In turn, the vast, non-extant Infant Jesus Hospital (1824–1826), built along the southern side of Świętokrzyska Street, defined the space of a new town square, known as Warecki (today: Powstańców Warszawy Square). Routes leading from the town were regulated and featured tollgate buildings, designed by Jakub Kubicki (two pairs of preserved buildings are situated in Unia Lubelska Square and Zamoyski Street).

The defeat of the November Uprising and a temporary halt to municipal investments were followed by several important realisations of considerable consequences for the development of the City. In 1860–1862, Krakowskie Przedmieście was widened by the demolishing of houses along the section from the statue of the Madonna of Passau to the Carmelite church. Special emphasis should be placed on the arrangement of Nowy Zjazd (a viaduct) from Castle Square towards the Vistula, and from here – towards the pontoon bridge. The author of Nowy Zjazd, built in 1844–1846, was engineer Feliks Pancer. Other undertakings included the marking of Kredytowa Street (1855–1856) and the regulation of Krucza Street, together with its side streets. Regulation was also carried out in the case of certain town squares, such as Saski, Za Żelazną Bramą and Grzybowski, a venture connected usually with the erection or redesigning of the large buildings fronting them, such as Saski (Saxon) Palace in Saski Square (1838–1842) or the bazaar known as Gościnny Dom in Za Żelazną Bramą Square (1841, destroyed in 1939).

Urban development spread mainly to the south and the west, and continued to remain enclosed by the former Lubomirski bulwarks. Generally speaking, in 1833–1864, permissions were granted for the erection of about 2 500 houses, the majority of these being built of brick.

Buildings with forms and decorations referring to historical styles, predominantly the Renaissance, began appearing in the first half of the nineteenth century. After a lengthy, almost century-long period of a decisive domination of secular architecture, the urban skyline now revealed new accents of church towers; the churches themselves became the spatial and plastic dominating elements of several Warsaw squares. In the seventeenth century, the architectural image of the town reflected the individuality of Tylman of Gameren, while the architect who left a very clear imprint of his talent on nineteenth-century Warsaw was the Italian-born Henryk Marconi. His works were inspired by outstanding Renaissance objects; hence, the characteristic features of the churches and buildings erected by him were a sophisticated combination of decorative motifs and carefully selected pro-

Powązki Communal Cemetery in Powązkowska Street; block of the Home Army "Zośka" battalion

Powązki Communal Cemetery in Powązkowska Street;
monument of Polish officers murdered in 1940 in Katyń

Powązki (Old) Cemetery, Avenue of Men of Merit;
quarter with graves of Polish actors

Powązki Communal Cemetery in Powązkowska Street; block of soldiers fallen in September 1939 during the defence of Warsaw

Evangelical Cemetery in Młynarska Street; the Bertold-Neuman family grave

Evangelical Cemetery in Młynarska Street

Moslem Cemetery in Młynarska Street

Powązki (Old) Cemetery, grave of composer Adam Minchejmer (1830–1904), executed by Antoni Oleszczyński and Bolesław Syrewicz

Russian Orthodox Cemetery
in Wolska Street

Б Т П
покоится прахъ
Дмитріевны
съ Дутовыхъ
браку Пашкевичъ
по 2му браку Мораки
скончав 16го Іюля 1889 г.
на 39 г. отъ роду
праху твоему!

portions. During the 1850s and at the beginning of the 1860s, the two imposing churches built according to projects by Marconi were St. Charles Borromeo in Chłodna Street (1841–1849) and All Souls in Grzybowski Square (in stages, from 1861). Marconi was also the author of the first railway station in Warsaw, situated in Jerozolimskie Avenue (1844–1845, partially pulled down prior to 1939), the first modern hotel – the "Europejski Hotel" in Krakowskie Przedmieście (in stages, from 1855), and the first building intended exclusively for offices – the Land Credit Society in Kredytowa Street (1856–1858).

During the first years after the January Uprising, spontaneous town development made use of empty building lots in central quarters, replacing old wooden houses and manors. Once those possibilities were exhausted, it turned to the open space, mainly to the south of Jerozolimskie Avenue and to the west of Karmelicka and Dzika streets. The progress of southbound development is testified by the fact that during the 1880s houses filled Krucza Street and its side streets; already at the turn of the nineteenth century, compact development spread along Polna and Marszałkowska streets towards Unia Lubelska Square. In order to facilitate communication and create access to the building plots, and thus facilitate their speculation, more than ten new streets were delineated and many old ones were extended.

The subdividing of land belonging to the former Infant Jesus Hospital was carried about around 1900. The resultant streets included Jasna, Moniuszko Sienkiewicz and Boduen. In the north-western part of the town, extensive divisions of land took place between Okopowa, Stawki, Gęsia and Dzika streets. In 1887, Miodowa Street, and in 1900, Karowa Street were linked with Krakowskie Przedmieście for the sake of more convenient communication. At the beginning of the twentieth century, a number of town squares: Zbawiciel (1901), Polytechnic (1902), Starynkiewicz (1902) and today's Narutowicz (1911) took on a shape that was to last until the second world war. In order to improve communication between Krakowskie Przedmieście and the riverside district of Powiśle, a viaduct named after Dr. Stanisław Markiewicz, and connected with Karowa Street, was built in 1903–1905.

The character and scale of housing development endowed Warsaw with a decidedly metropolitan appearance. At the end of the nineteenth century, the architecture of the town was dominated by eclectic solutions, combining assorted stylistic forms within a single object as well as earlier compositions referring to a certain historical style. The beginning of the twentieth century witnessed a brief supremacy of Art Nouveau, which gave way to monumental modernistic compositions. The streets of Warsaw were dominated by multi-storey houses, determining the character of the most important town arteries – Marszałkowska Street and its side streets, and Jerozolimskie Avenue. This type of housing appeared also in the historical Krakowskie Przedmieście and Nowy Swiat streets, producing a jarring aesthetic dissonance. Metropolitan accents were provided by imposing public utility buildings: the massive Main Post Office (destroyed during the war) in Warecki Square (1900), the "Under the Eagles" Bank, designed by Jan Heurich the Younger

The Wedel house in Szpitalna Street, erected in 1893 acc. to a project by Franciszek Braumann

The Hołowczyc house in Nowy Świat Street, erected in 1820 acc. to a project by Antonio Corazzi; reconstructed after wartime damage, 1949

Cooperative Societies Bank – the "Under the Eagles" house, built in 1912–1917 acc. to a project by Jan Heurich the Younger

←

House at the junction of Nowy Świat Street and Jerozolimskie Avenue

Church of St. Alexander in Trzech Krzyży Square; rebuilt after wartime devastation in 1949–1950 upon the basis of a project by Chrystian Piotr Aigner from 1818

→

196

"Sheraton" Hotel in Prusa Street, built in 1994–1996 acc. to a project by Tadeusz Spychała, Piotr Szaroszyk and team

The Poznański Palace in Ujazdowskie Avenue; reconstruction in 1949 referred to pre-1944 forms of the Palace, acc. to a project from 1859 by Franciszek Maria Lanci

The Sobański Palace in Ujazdowskie Avenue, built in 1852–1853 acc. to a project by Julian Ankiewicz

199

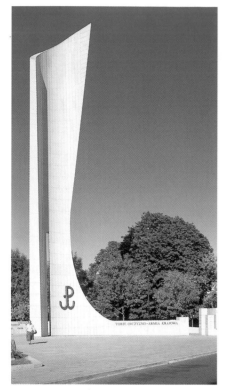

Monument of the Home Army and the Polish Underground State in front of the building of the Sejm (Parliament) in Wiejska Street, 1999, project by Jerzy Staniszkis

in Jasna Street (1912–1917), and the State Bank in Bielańska Street (1911). Monumental offices of banks and the Municipal Credit Society (1878–1880) were raised in Traugutt and Czacki streets. New hotels were built in Krakowskie Przedmieście – the "Bristol", designed by Marconi (1899–1901), and in Jerozolimskie Avenue – the "Polonia" (1909–1913).

Equally impressive seats were erected for scientific and cultural institutions – the Warsaw Polytechnic (1899–1901), the Philharmonic Hall in Jasna Street (1901), the "Zachęta" art exhibition hall in Małachowski Square (1898–1900), the Polski Theatre in Karasia Street (1912), the Krasiński Foundation Library in Okólnik Street, and the Municipal Library in Koszykowa Street (1914). The former town-planning configuration was seriously affected by a town investment consisting of the two Mirowska market halls, built in 1899–1902 on the line of the Saxon Axis.

Seats of industrial and financial potentates assumed the character of large palaces, such as the Kronenberg Palace, built by the outstanding Berlin architect J. H. F. Hitzig in Małachowski Square (1867–1871; demolished in 1961–1962) or the Szlenker Palace in Dąbrowski Square (1881–1883); elegant villas appeared along Ujazdowskie Avenue and the side streets leading to it.

Over ten new churches were raised in the city centre, including the church of the Saviour in Marszałkowska Street (1900–1911) and of St. Paul and Peter in Wspólna Street (1883–1886), Russian Orthodox churches, such as the cathedral in Saski Square (1894–1910; pulled down in 1921–1926), the Evangelical-Reformed church in Leszno (1866–1882), and Jewish prayer houses and synagogues, including the so-called Main Synagogue in Tłumackie (1877, demolished by the Nazis in 1943). The towers and domes of the new sacral objects created important accents in the panorama and the perspectives of the city streets. Height and monumental forms comprised characteristic traits of the multi-storey "Cedergren" building in Zielna Street (1904–1909).

The outstanding architects who designed the majority of the Warsaw buildings and churches included Leandro Marconi, Władysław Marconi, Jan Heurich the Younger, Stefan Szyller and Witold Lanci.

Not all of the newly erected and redesigned secular and sacral buildings met with the approval of the residents of Warsaw, displeased with the presence of Russian Orthodox churches and the architecture of Staszic Palace, partially redesigned in the "Byzantine" style (during the nineteenth century). Such forms and decoration, alien to Warsaw architectural tradition and associated with the cultural expansion of the partitioning power, introduced a strong dissonance into the image of the city.

The inter-war period brought primarily a rapid expansion of the capital beyond its historical centre. Nonetheless, development within the administrative limits of old Warsaw continued to fulfil the most important functions, providing employment, accommodation and concentrated services. A description of the town-planning and architectonic appearance of Warsaw, made by Jerzy Cegielski in 1920, noted: "From the aesthetic viewpo-

Main building of the Sejm of the Republic of Poland in Wiejska Street, erected in 1925–1928 acc. to a project by Kazimierz Skórewicz

Ujazdowski Castle, built in 1619–1624 acc. to a project by Giovanni Battista Trevano or Matteo Castelli; reconstructed from 1973

Ujazdowski Castle

Building of the Office of the Council of Ministers in Ujazdowskie Avenue, erected after 1900 acc. to a project by Wiktor J. Piotrowski and Henryk J. Gay

Statue of Ignacy Jan Paderewski in Ujazdowski Park, prior to 1939, project by M. Kamieński

The Belweder (Belvedere) Palace in Belwederska Street, built in about 1740, thoroughly redesigned in 1818–1822 acc. to a project by Jakub Kubicki

The "Under the Gryphons" house in Trzech Krzyży Square, erected in 1884–1886 acc. to a project by Józef Huss

→

204

House of the Association of Technicians (NOT) in Czacki Street, built in 1903–1905 acc. to a project by Jan Fijałkowski

Building of the Polski (Polish)
Bank in Bielańska Street,
built after 1900 acc. to a project
by Julian Ankiewicz, Piotr Frydrych
and Leontiy Nikolaevich Benois;
not reconstructed after wartime
devastation

Houses from the turn of the nineteenth
century in Lwowska Street
←

House of the former Warsaw
Municipal Credit Society in
Czacki Street, erected in 1878–1880
acc. to a project by Julian Ankiewicz
←

The "Atrium" office-trade complex in Jan Paweł II Street, erected in 1992–1995 acc. to a project by D. Fraser, T. Kazimierski and A. Ryba

The "Ściana Wschodnia" (Eastern Wall) commercial-residential complex in Marszałkowska Street, built in 1960–1969 acc. to a project by Z. Karpiński, J. Klewin

"Mercure" Hotel in Jan Paweł II Street, erected in 1991–1992 acc. to a project by Juliusz Roub

Monument "For Those who Perished and were Murdered in the East" in Muranowska Street, 1995, executed by Maksymilian Biskupski

"Centralny" train station in Jerozolimskie Avenue, built in 1972–1976 acc. to a project by Arseniusz Romanowicz and team

Jerozolimskie Avenue with the building of the "Polonia" Hotel (1909–1913) and the Art Nouveau Wilhelm Rakman house (1905–1906) at the corner of Poznańska Street

Palace of Science and Culture in Defilad Square, built in 1952–1955 acc. to a project by Lev V. Rudniev and team

←————————

Jerozolimskie Avenue with skyscrapers of the "Marriott" hotel, the Handlowy (Commercial) Bank and the FiM Tower Building

←————————

Main Building of the Warsaw Polytechnic, erected in 1899—1900 acc. to a project by Stefan Szyller

Pavilions of the Prince Józef Poniatowski bridge and viaduct, built in 1907–1913 acc. to a project by Stefan Szyller

Ujazdowski Park, created in 1893–1896 acc. to a project by Franciszk Szanior

222

Łazienkowska Motorway, built in 1971–1974

int, the City contrasted vividly with the surrounding suburbs: the stone island of the City towered above the empty spaces and the low housing, as a rule unplanned and semi-rural".

A quest for space for all the above mentioned functions was conducted mainly by the addition of new floors to old buildings and the erection of multi-storey edifices in the place of those demolished, as well as the development of the already scarce parks and gardens. The prime task was to meet the needs of state administration, science and culture. The city centre became the site of ministries and offices, banks, public utility institutions and housing estates for high-ranking state civil servants and academic professors (the estate in Myśliwiecka Street).

The architectural form of the majority of the state administration and public utility buildings and Roman Catholic churches erected at the time was maintained in the modernistic style, albeit in comparison with early twentieth-century modernism we may observe forms further simplified and a tendency towards rendering structural elements more legible. The most outstanding modernistic erections include the Domestic Administration Bank (1928–1931) in Jerozolimskie Avenue, designed by Rudolf Swierczyński, the Courts in Leszno (1935–1939), designed by Bohdan Pniewski, and the Ministry of Religion and Public Education (1925–1930) in Szuch Avenue, designed by Zdzisław Mączyński. For a rather long time, the main trend of modernistic architecture was accompanied by academic Classicism, present primarily in projects by the graduates of the St. Petersburg Academy: the Agricultural Bank in Nowogrodzka Street (1926–1928), designed by Marian Lalewicz. The basic components of this type of buildings were columnades, porticoes and classicizing frontages, designed in the spirit of modernism. At the same time, there appeared strong tendencies towards popularising historic Polish architecture, mainly Baroque, expressed in the Stefan Batory Secondary School, erected in 1922–1924 in Myśliwiecka Street, and designed by Tadeusz Tołwiński.

The characteristic features of Warsaw architecture of the interwar period were solid execution and luxurious interiors; good craftsmanship was appreciated, while building and decorative materials were selected carefully. Examples of such an approach include residential housing (e. g. 101 Jerozolimskie Avenue, 7 Lwowska Street, 7 Konopnicka Street, 69 Bartoszewicz Street and 10 Koszykowa Street).

Damage inflicted during the second world war affected predominantly the city centre. Almost 100 % of the area included into the ghetto was destroyed. The rest of the centre was burnt down, with the exception of houses used by the Germans, e. g. Jerozolimskie Avenue and its environs, and part of Krakowskie Przedmieście around the Presidential Palace. Postwar reconstruction led to the disappearance of entire fragments of the prewar city centre and the partial obliteration of the historical pattern of streets and squares. Apart from the above mentioned region of the ghetto, this process occurred predominantly among the most valuable nineteenth-century City complexes: entire blocks were pulled down due to the construc-

JOWISZ

tion of the Palace of Culture and Science (the area of Marszałkowska Street, Jerozolimskie Avenue, Emilia Plater and Świętokrzyska streets), and houses in the regions of the side streets of Służewska, Marszałkowska, Piękna and Koszykowa streets were demolished as a result of the construction of the Marszałkowska Residential District; the same fate befell the environs of Świętokrzyska, Królewska and Marszałkowska streets. Fortunately, the partially burnt, but rebuilt or reconstructed houses in Krakowskie Przedmieście, Nowy Świat Street and Ujazdowskie Avenue were preserved. Certain edifices (including residential housing) in the side streets of Marszałkowska Street (e. g. fragments of Wilcza, Nowogrodzka, Wspólna, Hoża and Żurawia streets) or the region of Wiejska and Na Dynasach streets were repaired.

The needs of the state administration inspired the erection of several hundred office buildings. Distinguished realisations included the Ministry of Communication in Chałubiński Street (1945–1950) and new parliamentary buildings in Wiejska Street (1948–1951), redesigned by Bohdan Pniewski, as well as the seat of the Economic Planning Commission in Trzech Krzyży Square (1948, designed by Stanisław Bieńkowski and Stanisław Rychlowski) and the Party Headquarters in Nowy Świat Street (1948–1951, designed by Wacław Tyszewski and team). Their characteristic traits include monumentalism and legible construction forms, despite tendencies towards blurring the latter by means of decorative elements. Interesting composition and modern solutions were, at the time of its construction, the features of the Main Statistical Office in Wawelska Street (1848–1954), built according to a project by Romuald Gutt.

Among the housing estates emerging in the city centre during this period the strongest impact upon the appearance of the town was exerted by Nowotko Street (today: General Władysław Anders Street) and the Marszałkowska Residential District with Konstytucji Square (1949–1952). The architecture of the new houses was dominated by forms propagated by the doctrine of socialist realism. Both the spatial conceptions and the composition of elevations and interiors referred to historical forms, mainly classically oriented, with attention drawn to the legibility of construction and function. On the other hand, attempts were made to introduce more modern technological methods and new, more resilient material.

Socialist realism did not eliminate other architectural tendencies, although the latter paved their way with difficulty in an atmosphere unfavourable for novel solutions. Functional and legible construction was the distinguishing feature of, among others, the Central Department Store (today: "Smyk") in Bracka Street (1948–1952), designed by Zbigniew Ihnatowicz.

The post-1956 period brought several realisations essential for the metropolitan image of the City, which fulfilled their functions satisfactorily. They were the Supersam building in Puławska Street (1960–1962, designed by Jerzy Hryniewecki) and the Peasant House in Powstancow Warszawy Square (1958–1961, designed by Bohdan Pniewski and Małgorzata Handzelewicz-Wacławkowa, with the cooperation of Wojciech Świątkowski).

Statue of "Jove" in Saski Garden, beginning of the 1730s, executed by Jan Jerzy Plersch

Zamkowy Square at night

The most important investment decisive for the further spatial shaping of the City consisted of housing projects built on the eastern side of Marszałkowska Street, between Jerozolimskie Avenue and Swiętokrzyska Street (1960–1969). A multi-functional complex along two communication lines was erected in Marszałkowska Street (municipal traffic) and the so-called city-centre passage behind department stores (pedestrians). The transparency of the spatial composition, the legibility of the structure of particular buildings and their functional assets place this complex amongst the more outstanding realisations in Poland. Naturally, a key place in architectural design which enhanced the image of the town in 1970–1980 was assumed by the reconstruction of the Royal Castle; enormous importance was attached also to modern communication routes and public utility objects, such as the Central railway station.

An important mark upon the architectural panorama of the city centre during the 1970s and the 1980s was made by new skyscrapers: the "Forum" Hotel (1972–1973) and office buildings in Stawki Street (1973–1975), as well as skyscrapers in the western region of the centre – the "Marriott" Hotel and the LOT terminal, enhancing the landscape of Warsaw. Skyscrapers placed against the backdrop of the Old Town disturb the panorama and must give rise to grave reservations. Other interesting realisations of the 1970s, which influenced the new appearance of Warsaw squares, include the "Victoria" Hotel in Piłsudski Square (1974–1976) and the effective composition of a bank façade in Powstańców Warszawy Square (1973–1974).

Bernardine (academic) church of St. Anne in Krakowskie Przedmieście Street at night

Bernardine (academic) church of St. Anne in Krakowskie Przedmieście Street at night

The 1980s – which witnessed the decline of the socialist economy – were a time of stagnation, and did not bring any significant spatial and architectural realisations. This was a lull preceding the investment boom of the 1990s. The present-day aerial view of the town is truly impressive: it would be difficult to count the cranes marking work on office buildings, banks, supermarkets and public utility buildings. The image of Central Warsaw changes in front of our eyes, giving rise not only to pleasure with the progress, but also to anxieties produced by the aesthetic and functionally justified selection of the accepted architectural and spatial proposals.Particular appreciation is shown to those which blend into the historical scale of their surroundings, such as the Sheraton Hotel (1994–1996) and the Holland Park building (1996–1998) in Trzech Krzyży Square, or the University Library, together with adjacent outbuildings, being erected in Powiśle. For the same reason, attention is attracted by the interesting realisations of office buildings in 8 Nowogrodzka Street and the so-called Zielna Point in Zielna Street (1997–1998). On the other hand, new skyscrapers in the urban panorama demonstrate rather schematic and monotonous architecture; even worse, they are erected in a situation of town-planning chaos, when very often the requirements and ambitions of emergent business ventures are the sole motivation for construction investments, irreversibly shaping town space.

The Presidential (Koniecpolski, Radziwiłł, Governor) Palace at night

Łazienkowska Motorway at night

Warsaw street lamps

Town Hall (the Jabłonowski Palace) in Teatralny Square, recreated in 1996–1997 by referring to

The ILMET skyscraper in ONZ (United Nations) Circle, built in 1994–1997 acc. to a project by Milenko Dumencic and Mirosław Kartowicz

The Royal Castle in Warsaw was always state property, and its royal resident was only a life-long user. This was the reason why the monarch, chosen in free elections, aimed at building his own private residence in Warsaw or its environs.

Such was the character of, among others, *Villa Regia*, raised and expanded by successive rulers from the Vasa dynasty during the first half of the seventeenth century, and later known as the Kazimierzowski Palace (named after King Jan Kazimierz); a similar function was fulfilled by a palace erected in Marymont at the end of the seventeenth century for Queen Maria Kazimiera, or the expansive (Saski) Saxon Palace, built by Augustus II and Augustus III during the first half of the eighteenth century.

In time, the majority of private regal residences were thoroughly redesigned, as was the case with the Kazimierzowski Palace or Saski Palace, destroyed during the second world war.

The two private royal residences which retained, to a large degree, their character and architectural features, are the palace-park complexes in Łazienki and Wilanów, both of exceptional artistic and historical value.

The beautiful terrain of the park-palace complex at Łazienki, situated in the very centre of Warsaw, is associated with the oldest history of the capital. As we recall from the history of the spatial development of the town, it was precisely here, on a hillock near the present-day astronomical laboratory, that traces of a settlement from the seventh century were found together with fragments of a castle-town connected with the dukes of Mazovia   Siemowit and his son, Konrad II, and dated as being thirteenth-century. Despite the fact that the two rulers transferred their seat to a place which subsequently became the site of the town of Warsaw, the terrains of Ujazdów did not cease fulfilling residential functions, especially from 1526, when Mazovia was incorporated into the Crown and Ujazdów became royal property. The famous Queen Bona, wife of King Zygmunt the Old, erected a large wooden manor, which became the centre of court life and the stage of numerous ceremonies. The manor was surrounded by an exceptionally magnificent Italian garden. The area of Ujazdów was inherited from her mother by Queen Anna the Jagiellon, whose reign also brimmed with significant events. Their peak moment were the ceremonies connected with the wedding of Jan Zamoyski and Katarzyna Radziwiłł, held in January 1578, when *Odprawa posłów greckich* (The Dismissal of Greek Envoys) by Jan Kochanowski was staged at Ujazdów Castle in the presence of the royal couple – Stefan Batory and Anna the Jagiellon. The picturesqueness and attractiveness of this site inclined King Zygmunt III to build an imposing palace (1624), known as Ujazdów Castle. The outline of the Castle, with four corner turrets and a characteristic steep roof, became an essential element in the Warsaw panorama, seen from the Vi-

Royal Residences at Łazienki and Wilanów

237

Wilanów Palace, elevation facing the garden, sopraporta with Sybil

←

White Cottage in the Łazienki Park, erected in 1774–1777 acc. to a project by Domenico Merlini

stula, and one of the best examples of the Vasa style, with its severe outer form. At the foot of the Castle, extensive lands stretching towards the river were occupied by a royal zoological garden, set up already at the end of the sixteenth century, and devoted to the breeding and study of animals. The interesting report made in 1596 by one of the secretaries of Zygmunt III probably refers to the Ujazdów zoo:

After dinner, the Cardinal set off to see the royal zoological garden, located two miles from Warsaw (...) We arrived at an enormous fenced-in forest, where various species of wild beasts, such as bisons, bears, boars, stags, deer, etc. are kept. In the centre, there stood a high gazebo, from which we could observe the animals without any danger.

Upon the basis of a parliamentary resolution of 1683, the Ujazdów estates were granted to Stanisław Herakliusz Lubomirski, one of the most powerful and outstanding magnates of the Commonwealth of Two Nations, who commissioned the renowned architect

Statue of Frederic Chopin in the Łazienki Park, replica of a sculpture by Wacław Szymanowski from 1904

239

Myślewicki Palace in the Łazienki Park, built in 1775–1778 acc. to a project by Domenico Merlini

Statue of **Satyr Striking a Cymbal** *on the southern terrace of the Palace on the Water in Łazienki, 1773–1778, executed by André Le Brun (copy of a classical sculpture)*

Temple of Sybil (Diana) in the Łazienki Park, erected prior to 1822

Łazienki Park

⟶

Palace on the Water in Łazienki, northern façade, 1787–1788, project by Jan Chrystian Kamsetzer

⟶

Palace on the Water, southern façade, 1784–1788, project by Domenico Merlini

Amphitheatre (Theatre on the Isle) in the Łazienki Park, erected in 1788–1791 acc. to a project by Jan Chrystian Kamsetzer

Decorative vase on a terrace in front of the Palace on the Water in Łazienki, end of the eighteenth century

244

Palace on the Water, fragment of an overdoor

Tylman of Gameren to redesign the interior of Ujazdów Castle and to establish a garden, together with pavilions. This was the origin of the future Palace on the Water – a pavilion containing a luxury bathroom. Up to this day, the Łazienki Palace is composed of interiors with Baroque decoration: an antechamber, known as the Bacchus Room, and a Bathroom. The visitors were greeted by an extant Latin inscription, which proclaimed: "This house hates sadness, loves peace, offers baths, recommends a pastoral life, and wishes to play host to honest people". The Bathroom, with preserved stucco reliefs depicting scenes from the *Metamorphoses* by Ovid, whose themes match the site, is of exceptional beauty. It was precisely this object which inspired the name of the pavilion and, subsequently, the entire palace-park complex.

A consecutive stage in the development of the Łazienki complex is represented by the years 1720–1763, when Łazienki and Ujazdów were leased by the Lubomirski family to Augustus II and Augustus III. The latter monarch enlarged the area of the former zoo and embarked upon a thorough expansion of the layout. The only significant trace of their activity is the so-called Piaseczyński Canal, which up to this day lies on the axis of Ujazdów Castle and follows a course from the escarpment to the Vistula.

The reign of Stanisław Augustus signified the climactic development of the entire complex. The last King of Poland purchased the land of the former zoological garden from the Lubomirski family immediately after ascending the throne in 1764. The first intention of the monarch was to redesign and expand the former Ujazdów Castle into an official royal residence, and to create around it an extensive spatial layout. Despite the fact that for financial reasons the King was forced to resign from his ambitious projects, the area in question, together with numerous buildings, became the site of his favourite residence. He arrived in Łazienki with his entire court directly after his name day, i. e. 8 May, and stayed until October. Work on the adaptation of the former zoo into a landscape park, as well as the transformation of garden buildings and pavilions and the erection of new ones, progressed in stages. During the first phase – 1774–1780 – a storey was added over the former Lubomirski bath, the so-called Myślewicki Palace was erected, and a charming small garden pavilion, known as the White Cottage, was built. Architectural ventures were pursued according to designs by Domenico Merlini, the court architect, while the rich painted decoration, primarily in the Myślewicki Palace and the White Cottage, were executed by Jan Bogumił Plersch. During the second stage, from 1784 to 1788, the most important work was conducted on the southern elevation of the Palace on the Water, endowed with refined form and a characteristic four-columnned portico. At the same time, the Old Orangery building, with a theatre hall in the eastern wing, was created. Untouched by time and reconstruction, it has survived to this day in the form and with the decorations designed by Merlini and Plersch, remaining one of the few prese-

Bridge and statue of King Jan III Sobieski, 1788, executed by Franciszek Pinck acc. to a project by André Le Brun

rved Neoclassical theatre interiors in Europe. A further expansion of the Palace on the Water was initiated in 1788 according to projects by Merlini and Jan Chrystian Kamsetzer, and completed as late as 1795. The new northern elevation displayed greater simplicity, linear qualities and compositional discipline than its southern counterpart. The most beautiful interiors include the Dining Room, the Picture Gallery, the Solomon Chamber, the Rotunda, and the Ballroom.

The Dining Room possesses enchanting ambience, excellent proportions and a charmingly contrasting arrangement of white and red stucco. Thanks to its legible composition, this interior holds a special place among the Merlini realisations, which observe rather more differentiated composition and colour configurations. The Dining Room became a permanent part of the history of Polish culture as the site of "Thursday dinners" (*obiady czwartkowe*) – meetings held by scholars and men of letters, hosted by the King.

The Picture Gallery was arranged by Jan Chrystian Kamsetzer for the purposes of displaying superior works of art selected from among the 2 300-strong royal painting collection. The canvases were featured in frames specially designed for the Gallery, and shown in a crowded arrangement, sometimes in several rows. The Gallery offered an opportunity for admiring renowned compositions by Rembrandt: *The Polish Rider, The Jewish Fiancee* and *Father of the Fiancee*. Today, *The Polish Rider* is displayed in the acclaimed Frick Collection in New York, and the two other Rembrandt paintings comprise one of the chief attractions of the Royal Castle in Warsaw. The most vivid accent in the Gallery is a fireplace of black marble and a medallion with a likeness of Antinous, hanging above it.

The most imposing interior is the so-called Solomon Chamber, named after a series of paintings illustrating the life of the Biblical king. The paintings, all of which were unfortunately destroyed during the second world war, praised King Stanisław Augustus, whom Bacciarelli depicted in the guise of Solomon. Other figures shown in the compositions also bore the features of members of the closest milieu of the Polish ruler. The composition of this Chamber, which blended the paintings with lavish decoration, gilt stucco and the opulence of the uniform interior design, is characteristic for representative interiors maintained in the Stanislavian style, envisaged similarly to the Royal Castle interiors.

The central part of the Palace contains a two-storey rotunda, designed by Merlini and situated precisely in the same spot as the grotto, with a centrally placed fountain, in the Lubomirski bathing pavilion. The appearance of the new interior was determined by colourful arrangements of stucco and marble. Niches contained statues of Polish monarchs: Kazimierz the Great, Stefan Batory, Zygmunt the Old and Jan III Sobieski. In turn, busts of three Roman emperors: Trajan, Titus and Marcus Aurelius, stood over the passages, and allegories of Wisdom, Valour, Justice and Mercy were executed by Marcello Bacciarelli on the

Palace on the Water, fragment of an overdoor

Wilanów Palace seen from the approach, built in stages from 1677 to 1696, expanded by adding wings in 1723–1732

Wilanów Palace, elevation facing the garden, sopraporta with Sybil

dome topping the interior. The message of this room is legible and clear-cut — its author wished to accentuate the value of governance based on honourable Polish tradition and on models of the ancient Roman system of rule.

In the western part of the Palace, Jan Chrystian Kamsetzer designed and added a two-storey, rectangular Ballroom. The architectural, sculpted and painted decoration of this simple and sparse interior referred to known classical and Renaissance models, e. g. the arabesque by Raphael in the Vatican Loggie. Statues of Apollo the Belvedere and Hercules Farnese stood on the mantelpieces.

The opulent painted and sculpted decoration of the Ballroom was composed according to an ideological programme, meticulously devised to the slightest detail, and referring to the reign of Stanisław Augustus, which, in accordance with the premises of the programme's authors, was conceived as comparable with the flourishing, mythical Golden Age.

A building distinct in the Łazienki Park, and erected in 1790–1791 according to a project by Kamsetzer, is the Amphitheatre, also known as the Theatre on the Isle. Its ceremonial opening took place on 7 September 1781 during the staging of an historical ballet entitled *Cleopatra*. The cockpit of the theatre is patterned on the Herculanum amphitheatre, and the stage — on the ruins of the temple of Jove in Baalbek (Lebanon). A highly original separation of the stage from the audience by means of water, and the introduction into the stage decoration of the surrounding natural landscape enabled Kamsetzer to achieve a work of high artistic rank. The Łazienki Amphitheatre is one of the few buildings of this type in the world.

Alltold, in not quite twenty years Stanisław Augustus created one of the most interesting park-palaces complexes in Europe, whose final character could be described as a villa-museum. Direct inspiration for the royal conceptions was sought in famous Italian villas, such as Villa Borghese, Villa Albani, Villa Medici or Villa Ludovisi, which amassed valuable works of classical and modern art. Thanks to accounts by artists, specially sent to Italy, and numerous published etchings the Polish monarch was familiar with the nature of the furnishing and functioning of Roman villas-museums.

The search for conceptions to be applied for the expanding Łazienki was influenced also by the experiences of English collectors and aesthetes, at the time decisive for European aesthetics in general.

During the nineteenth century, the Łazienki complex, shaped by Stanisław Augustus, continued to be regarded as one of the most attractive sites in Warsaw. In 1817, it became imperial property and, together with the nearby Belvedere Palace, served as a seat for Grand Duke Constantine.

The area between the former large outbuilding (known also as Podchorążówka, from the Cadet School located here during the period of the Kingdom of Poland) and the Belvedere formed a stage for the first act of the November Uprising of 1831, when the cadets attacked the residence of the Grand Duke.

Throughout the entire nineteenth century, the park remained open to the public, and became the representative "salon" of Warsaw. It continued to hold this status in the reborn Polish state, frequently serving as a residence for the guests of the President of the Republic of Poland.

In the wartime period, the majority of buildings remained unharmed, with the exception of the Palace on the Water, burned down during the Uprising of 1944. Rebuilt after the war, it is, together with other objects and the park, the central element of one of the most magnificent museum complexes in Poland.

The palace-garden premise in Wilanów, situated in the southern part of Warsaw, several kilometres from the town centre, is much earlier than Łazienki. The origin of the Wilanów residence go back to 1677, when Jan III Sobieski, the recently elected King of the Commonwealth of Two Nations, decided to build a summer residence in the Milanów estate. The name of the extensive property was changed to Villa Nuova, subsequently giving rise to its Polish version of Wilanów. The Wilanów complex is certainly the most outstanding among the artistic accomplishments of the patronage of Jan III Sobieski, and the high assessment of its artistic merit is confirmed by excellent architecture, both of the original manor and the later villa and palace. Wilanów Palace was erected in stages. Despite the fact that it was an embodiment of an ideal gentry residence, the brick manor, raised in 1677–1679, proved too modest for the requirements of a royal court; already in 1681–1688 it was given an additional mezzanine, while both façades were granted a new Baroque architectonic form, with lavish stucco decorations. The building owes its monumental character predominantly to the composition of the elevation, rendered uniform by means of the introduction of galleries, linking the main corps with the square towers. In this way, the manor assumed the character of a truly representative edifice, displaying all the features of an Italian villa. The author of the three stages in the development of the Wilanów residence during the reign of Jan III Sobieski was Augustyn Locci the Younger, the royal architect who cooperated with a group of Italian stucco decorators, the celebrated sculptor Andreas Schlüter of Gdańsk, the sculptor Stefan Szwaner and a number of painters headed by Jerzy Eleutner Siemiginowski and Michelangelo Palloni. All those artists transferred to the façades of the Wilanów villa a sophisticated ideological programme, presenting the principles of monarchic rule devised at the court of Louis XIV. Not until the end of the monarch's life did Wilanów Palace, in its complete form, become a true monument to the glory of the victor at the siege of Vienna. Furthermore, each phase in the development of the residence entailed work on the villa surrounding. An extensive parade courtyard, situated before the front elevation, was preceded by a courtyard entered

Wilanów Palace, the "Pogoń" coat of arms of the Grand Duchy of Lithuania on the garden elevation

Wilanów, entrance gate to palace courtyard, 1689

Wilanów, palace park

Wilanów, mausoleum of Stanisław Kostka and Aleksandra Potocki, built in 1836 acc. to a project by Henryk Marconi

Wilanów Palace, northern gallery from the front

Wilanów Palace, medallion from the Famous Women *series on the garden elevation*

through an imposing extant gate. A geometrical garden, created on the other side of the palace, is composed of spheres, stalls and espaliers, descending in terraces towards the old river bed of the Vistula. Reconstructed after the second world war, this garden relates to the original, Baroque complex. The architecture of the villa was maintained in the Italian artistic tradition, but the park was inspired by Italian and French conceptions of park-palace complexes. At the turn of the 1680s, the last stage in the expansion of the Wilanów royal residence consisted of the addition of a large storey above the central part of the residence and topping the towers with high lanterns. These innovations altered the character of the building, which from that time could be called a palace, albeit truly palace-like features were created only after thorough redesigning in the 1730s, when two long wings were added to the existing corpus on both sides of the courtyard. In this way, there came into being a characteristic layout on the plan of a horseshoe, the work of the court of Augustus II.

Visitors to the Sobieski residence in Wilanów are struck primarily by the beauty of the location, the refined solid and the sophisticated proportions of the palace. Approaching it more closely, they are surprised to discover an extraordinary richness of architectonic detail as well as sculpted and painted compositions, which form interesting albeit complicated thematic motifs. The programme of the front elevation, full of references to ancient mythology, focuses on a basic theme, namely, the glorification of the ruler. In turn, the intention behind the programme of decorating the garden elevation is to depict the Wilanów residence as the seat of Apollo, the Sun-King.

Historians of architecture draw attention to the impetus of Wilanów Palace, the architectural and decorative programme of its elevations, as well as the outfitting of the interiors of the regal seat, which, as regards contents and stylistic qualities, precedes all other Polish residences dating from the end of the seventeenth century.

Despite subsequent alterations, quite a lot of the original furnishing of the Wilanów interiors has survived. They constitute the greatest tourist attraction, admired for their state of preservation and suitable conservation. All the representative rooms are located on the ground floor of the Palace, and were spatially composed in accordance with the sixteenth-century tradition of residential architecture. In this configuration, a fundamental role is played by interiors situated along the axis of the layout, which in Wilanów are represented by the Great Vestibule and the Dutch Study. Along both sides of the central interiors are two identical complexes of chambers, comprising the apartments of the King and the Queen. In accordance with the principle of composing and planning residential interiors, accepted at European courts of the period, each apartment should have consisted of an antechamber, a bedroom and two or three small studies. This is the case also in Wilanów, where an antechamber and a bedroom adjoin three small studies. In turn, the upper storey of Wilanów Palace contains more modest apartments, intended for the royal family. The aforementioned superstructure, creating a lofty floor above the central part of the Palace, contained the Great Chamber, which probably served numerous representative functions, such as court banquets; hence, it is known up to this day as the Great Banquet Hall of Jan III Sobieski.

Although redesigned at the beginning of the nineteenth century, the Great Vestibule retained several elements of the original outfitting, including allegories of the four elements on the facette. It seems worth recalling that at the time of Jan III an equestrian statue of the King stood in the centre of the hall, granting it a commemorative character by referring to his martial deeds.

Considerably more of the original seventeenth-century decoration is to be found in the apartments of the King and the Queen. The King's Bedroom includes a well preserved plafond, executed by Siemiginowski, and depicting *Summer*, as well as a lavish stucco-painted decoration of the bed-moulding and window jambs, with the prevailing motifs of maritime fauna. The Queen's Bedroom is dominated by a plafond showing an allegory of *Spring*, and the bed-moulding contains admirable and equally opulent stucco-painted decorations, with the motifs of sphinxes. The ideological programme, concentrated around allegories of the four seasons, is expressed in *Autumn*, in the Queen's Antechamber and *Winter*, in the King's Antechamber, both painted by Siemiginowski.

Attention is drawn particularly to the programme featured in the King's Library, with plafonds depicting allegories of Theology and Philosophy, as well as portraits of learned men and artists, such as Nicolaus Copernicus. In the *al fresco* Study Siemiginowski executed his best works – likenesses of Apollo and Sibyl as well as Apollo as a shepherd.

Much more modest are the apartments of the royal family situated on the mezzanine of the Palace. Several interiors, however, preserved interesting painted and stucco decorations, the most beautiful being the ceiling in the Porcelain Study and the polychromy on the walls and ceiling of the so-called Quiet Room.

Separate place among the artistic achievements of the court of Jan III Sobieski is held by the decoration of both garden galleries joining the main corps of the Palace with the towers, and executed by the painter Michelangelo Palloni and a group of Italian stucco artists. The topic of the painting, unfortunately very badly damaged in certain places, is the *History of Amor and Psyche.*

After the death of Jan III, the Wilanów residence remained the property of the Sobieski family (to 1720), and then frequently changed hands. In 1720–1729, it belonged to Elżbieta Sieniawska, nee Lubomirska, one of the richest women in the Commonwealth, and from 1729 to 1799, with a brief interval when it was leased by King Augustus II, it was the residence of the Czartoryski and Lubomirski families. In

Wilanów Palace, sundial on the garden elevation

1799–1892, Wilanów belonged to the Potockis. The last owners, prior to the nationalisation of Wilanów, were the Branicki family (1892–1945).

While in Wilanów, it is worth paying attention to the Bath House and the Kitchen, built in 1775–1778 according to a design by Szymon Bogumił Zug, their plain forms contrasting with the Baroque Palace. The neo-Gothic mausoleum of Stanisław and Aleksandra Potocki, built in 1836 by Henryk Marconi and with a splendid statue by Jakub Tatarkiewicz, stands in front of the Palace. Marconi also designed the imposing neo-Renaissance parish church of St. Anne, erected in 1857–1870. The only part of the former Riding School to have remained is its neo-historical façade from 1848–1859; the modern building concealed behind it houses the Poster Museum.

Apart from the earlier mentioned oldest park at Wilanów with its characteristic regular pattern, visitors may enjoy an English park, situated to the north of the Palace, and a part of an English-Chinese park as well as a charming neo-Renaissance garden in front of the southern wing of the Palace.

Despite the fact that in the course of the last two centuries many interesting architectural and garden works appeared in the Wilanów complex, they did not alter essentially the artistic character of the residence of the vanquisher-king.

Fate protected the Wilanów complex from wartime damage, and after thorough restoration, conducted in 1955–1965, as a museum, featuring valuable collections, and the exceptional garden-palace complex it attracts hundreds of thousands of tourists annually.

Wilanów Palace, Chronos, fragments of the sundial on the garden elevation

Wilanów Palace, spire of palace tower

*U*ntil 1918, the development of Warsaw rarely extended beyond the bulwarks built in 1770. From the Early Middle Ages, areas which today resound with the metropolitan life of districts surrounding the City, included numerous ducal and gentry villages. Solec, Powązki, Półków, Młociny, Buraków, Wielka Wola or Jazdów were ducal property, while Raków belonged to the gentry, and the village of Mokotów – to various owners, including the Church. In 1575–1764, particular renown was enjoyed by the village of Wielka Wola, where eleven elections of Polish kings were held.

Spatial growth beyond the boundaries of the Old and the New Towns encompassed vast terrains, from Wilanów in the south, Bielany in the north, and Wola in the west. Intensified settlement occurred after the ultimate transference of the official royal residence from Cracow to Warsaw, i. e. in about 1619. This was the period of the origin of suburban residences, among which pride of place went to Ujazdów Castle, built by Zygmunt III. The gentry, the clergy, and, more rarely, the burghers, founded their seats in the present-day districts of Mokotów, Okęcie, Włochy, Rakowiec, and Szczęśliwice. In 1639, Władysław IV settled the Camaldolites further to the north of the town (today: Bielany), where they erected a wooden church and a monastery.

The settlement movement to the north of the New Town spread across lands close to the road leading to Zakroczym and on the Vistula escarpment. The largest development included the landed estates of Primate Mikołaj Prażmowski, the Parys, Samborski and Wołczyński gentry families, as well as the Dominicans and the Paulites. Further to the north, in the region where the Drna flowed into the Vistula, there stretched the landed estate of the Holy Ghost Hospital, and even further – the manor of the village of Półków, which from 1641 was the property of the Camaldolites from Bielany.

The end of the seventeenth century signified lively activity predominantly in the extensive territories of Jazdów, Czerniaków, and Lower Mokotów, where Stanisław Herakliusz Lubomirski, Grand Marshal of the Crown, commissioned buildings erected by the architect Tylman of Gameren. The resultant complex including such as the ornamental pavilion in the Ujazdów zoological garden, containing a bath (1683–1689) – the embryo of the future Łazienki Palace – or the Bernardine church in Czerniaków (1689–1693) created important spatial accents, contributing to a transformation of the character of this part of the town.

Further to the south, in the village of Milanów, Jan III Sobieski established a summer residence, which he named Wilanów (Villa Nuova). Originally (about 1680), the core of the future palace-park complex was a small manor, which, having been expanded in 1681–1682, assumed the appearance of an Italian villa, and after successive extension in 1692 received the character of a palace. The Wilanów residence encompassed a large area, becoming an essential spatial element of the southern re-

Building next to the royal spring in Zakroczymska Street, built in the first quarter of the eighteenth century, redesigned in 1771

259

gions of Warsaw. In turn, in the northern part of the city, Queen Maria Kazimiera created a small summer residence known as Marie-mont, in tribute to her, which gave rise to today's Marymont.

Among the Warsaw town-planning schemes from the first half of the eighteenth century a significant impact on the further shaping of the City was exerted by the so-called Saxon Axis and Kalwaryjska Route; the third, Gwardii Avenue, leading from the New Town to the barracks of the Crown Foot Guards – in the present-day area of the Citadel – was less significant. It lost its importance due to nineteenth-century demolitions, which were the outcome of the construction of the Citadel. Before this took place, the Avenue constituted an important urbanising element in the northern part of Warsaw – i. e. the future Żoliborz district. During the reign of Stanisław Augustus, newly delineated plots were purchased by the most prosperous burghers, bankers, traders and the gentry. The streets of Żoliborz were laid out according to a plan devised by geometricians, who adapted old routes leading to the north. To the south, the emergent district was restricted by the gorge of the Bałcząca rivulet, while the northern boundary was the Drna. To the west, regulation reached the later Pokorna Street. The main streets of the new district: Gwardii Avenue, which became Fawory and Zielona streets, diverged at the confluence of Zakroczymska and Spadek streets.

Only towards the west did the division of town land cross the line of the Marshal Lubomirski bulwarks, created in 1770, by encompassing Wielka Wola, located along a road leading to the small town of Błonie. In 1775, this land, which at the beginning of the reign of Stanisław Augustus belonged to Alojzy Fryderyk Brühl, became the property of the infamous magnate Adam Poniński. The latter divided part of his terrains into plots, which he leased; in the environs of the bulwarks he established the Wola jurisdiction and built a palace. Several *włóki* (1 *włóka* = 30 *morgi*, 1 *mórg* = 6 578 sq. yards) were bought by the banker Karol Schultz, who erected a suburban residence in Karolkowa Street, delineated southwards from the Wola highroad. A large number of mills was built along Młynarska Street, perpendicular to the Wola Tract. Brick kilns situated near the Czyste delineated estate were reached by a newly marked street, known as Przyokopowa. The main street in this part of the suburbs was the Wola road, which adjoined farm land. Its boundary was composed of streets between the Wola Tract and a tract leading to the villages of Babice and Gorce (later: Górczewska Street). In this manner, the town planning process in Wielka Wola and adjacent landed estates gave rise to the future industrial district of Warsaw.

From the viewpoint of the utilisation of terrains directly associated with the town, a noteworthy event was the issuing of a decree on the closure of church cemeteries in Warsaw and the transference of burials outside the city limits. A cemetery intended for the parishes of the New and the Old Towns was established near the village of Powązki, immediately behind the Lubomirski bulwark. The Evangelical-Augsburg cemetery was ope-

Statue of the Mermaid on the Kościuszko Embankment, 1939, executed by Ludwika Nitschowa

ned in Młynarska Street, an Evangelical-Reformed cemetery – at the crossroads of Młynarska and Żytnia streets, and a Jewish cemetery behind present-day Okopowa Street. All three cemeteries have continued to fulfil their functions to this very day.

Changes in the appearance of the town were accomplished also by extensive parks, introduced within its range and environs and designed under the impact of fashionable English and French solutions. The central point of the composition of such a premise was usually a small palace, as in Mokotów or Natolin near Warsaw. The picturesque parks, designed mainly by Szymon Bogumił Zug, contained copies of classical buildings alongside neo-Gothic pavilions, and mosques next to rural thatch-roofed cottages. This was the way Princess Izabella Czartoryska planned Powązki (in the region of present-day Dolnośląska Street, Elbląska Street and Izabella Street), and Princess Izabella Lubomirska – Mokotów (remnants in Puławska Street). Old Baroque park layouts, such as Łazienki, Natolin and Wilanów, were transformed and extended.

The aforementioned erection of the Citadel in the northern part of town (1832-1836) had considerable consequences for the spatial development of Warsaw; its construction absorbed but largely destroyed the district of Fawory and halted development along the Vistula.

Despite dynamic demographic growth and a considerable elevation of the city's economic standing during the second half of the nineteenth century, its development remained enclosed within the boundaries of today's city centre. Not until the beginning of the twentieth century were Solec and the terrains between Czerniakowska Street, Podchorążych Street and Belwederska Street divided into plots, thus delineating Chełmska Street and its most important side streets. After 1911, over ten side streets of present-day Puławska Street in Upper Mokotów were delineated, including Rakowiecka, Narbutt, Madaliński and Szuster streets. To the west, this quarter was closed by Wołoska Street. In the Ochota district, the division of land was carried out between Niemcewicz, Szczęśliwicka and Grójecka streets. Larger industrial enterprises were situated in the Wola, Powiśle and Praga districts. The Jewish population lived mainly in quarters in the north-western part of Warsaw. Nonetheless, despite such intense land division, the suburban areas outside the city limits remained semi-rural.

As has been mentioned, the regaining of independence by Poland in 1918 and the assumption of the functions of a capital signified a breakthrough in the spatial history of Warsaw and its City. Warsaw now spread beyond its traditional boundaries. The town planning of the new districts was inspired by the idea of a garden suburb (Sadyba, Żoliborz). Its derivatives were town planning premises whose central point was a circular or semicircular square, crossed by an important communication artery (Narutowicz Square, Wilson Square, Inwalidów /Invalides'/ Square).

The modern residential estates which appeared during this period included the particularly noteworthy Warsaw Housing Cooperative in Żoli-

The Gniński (Ostrogski) Palace, reconstructed in 1949–1954 by referring to pre-1944 forms of the Palace, project by Tylman of Gameren

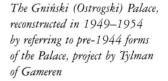

Monument of the Military Action of Polish emigrants in America in Wojska Polskiego Avenue, project by Andrzej Pityński

Statue of Jan Matejko in Puławska Street, acc. to a project by Marian Konieczny, 1989

Monument "Killed-Invincible 1939–1945", acc. to a project by K. Zemło, unveiled in 1973, park in Sowiński Street

The Electio Viritim *obelisk commemorating the Election Field in the Wola District, situated at the junction of Płocka, Obozowa and Ostroroga streets, 1996–1997, executed by Stanisław Michalik*

Plate with an eagle, fragment of the Citadel Execution Gate

borz. Starting with 1922, the terrain on the eastern side of Mickiewicz Street, between Inwalidów Square, Wojska Polskiego Avenue, the Citadel and Krasiński Square was filled with clusters of small villas built by an Army Cooperative, known as "Officers' Żoliborz". A "Civil Servants' Żoliborz" was created on the other side of Mickiewicz Street, between Inwalidów Square, Wojska Polskiego, Wyspiański and Krasiński streets. In 1928–1939, a journalists' cooperative estate was built between Krasiński, Sułkowski, Karpiński and Dziennikarska streets, and at the beginning of the 1930s an estate was created by a cooperative of the Institute of Social Security. The largest housing estate, built from 1927 to the outbreak of the second world war, was the aforementioned estate of the Warsaw Housing Cooperative. The area between Wilson Square and Krasiński, Stołeczna and Słowacki streets was occupied by nine housing developments. The architectural avant-garde of the capital comprised Bohdan Lachert, Jerzy Szanajca, Barbara and Stanisław Brukalski, and Juliusz Żórawski, authors of the majority of the modern estates and villas. Finally, residential housing appeared on the eastern side of Słowacki Street, all the way to Gdańska Street. In Bielany, gradual development encompassed the area between Żeromski Street, Podczaszyński Street, Konstytucji Avenue and Kasprowicz Street.

In the Ochota district, the years 1924–1926 witnessed the development of the area between present-day Wielkopolski park and Narutowicz Square, which became the so-called Lubecki Project; the so-called Staszic Project was built on the eastern side of the park, along Filtrowa Street – between today's Krzywicki Street and Niepodległości Avenue (after 1922). The second large estate of the Warsaw Housing Cooperative, after Żoliborz, was built in 1931–1936 in Rakowiec, between Wiślicka and Pruszkowska streets.

A number of housing projects was created in Mokotów, in an area defined by Rakowiecka, Wołoska, Madaliński and Puławska streets. Land between Puławska Street was divided into building plots, as was the area on its eastern side – between Unii Lubelskiej Avenue to Dolna Street, and the western side – as far as Naruszewicz Street. In 1924, the Sadyba cooperative estate in Czerniaków was designed along both sides of Powsińska Street, next to the fort. New houses appeared along a section of Belwederska Street between Parkowa and Podchorążych streets, on the western side of Belwederska Street (the so-called Grottger Project).

In Wola, land division took place between Wolska, Młynarska, Płocka and Dworska streets, as well as in Koło, where houses of the Society of Workers' Estates were built.

Parks created in the new districts included the Sowiński in Wola, Dreszer in Mokotów, Żeromski in Żoliborz, and Maria Curie-Skłodowska and Wielkopolski in Ochota. In 1934, Bielany Woods were incorporated into the town, and in 1938 the city council purchased the Kabaty Woods.

The wartime period, which destroyed the city centre almost totally, to a large measure spared districts situated beyond it. It was there that the

Warsaw University New Library in Dobra Street, built in 1994–1999 acc. to a project by Marek Budzyński and Zbigniew Badowski

Alexander Citadel, Iwanowska Gate (Execution Gate), erected in 1832–1836 acc. to a project by Ivan Dehn

population grew the quickest immediately after the war, and that the first postwar housing estates were to appear, e. g. in Żoliborz, Mokotów, and Wola.

When in 1951 extensive suburban estates and settlements became part of Warsaw, they assumed the role of sites of industrial enterprises (e. g. in Służewiec) or new housing estates. The first large housing estates, e. g. Bielany II–IV, originated in 1957–1965, or after 1965 – Młociny and Stegny. Among the estates designed and built during this period the only distinctive one is Sady Żoliborskie (Żoliborz Orchards, after 1960).

An important role in spatial development plans was played by open terrains intended for recreation and leisure. This was the time of the origin of multi-functional parks in Kępa Potocka, Moczydło or Szczęśliwice.

An important investment was the new Airport in Okęcie (1964–1969, expanded in 1990–1992), which enhanced the attractiveness of land along Żwirko and Wigura Avenue and its side streets, especially after

Estate of the Seventh Warsaw Housing Cooperative in the Żoliborz district, built in 1932 acc. to a project by Barbara and Stanisław Brukalski

Residential house in Katowicka Street in the Saska Kępa district, erected in 1928–1929 acc. to a project by Bohdan Lachert and Józef Szanajca

Villa belonging to Barbara and Stanisław Brukalski in Niegolewski Street in the Żoliborz district, built by the owners in 1927–1928

The Szuster Palace in Puławska Street; the original building was erected in 1772–1774; the present-day form is the result of redesigning in 1822–1825 acc. to a project by Henryk Marconi

Monument of Martyrs of Communist Terror 1944–1956 in Fosa Street, 1992–1993 executed by Maciej Szańkowski

"Yellow Inn", about 1846, project by F.M. Lanci

1989. The important exit arteries of Kasprzak Street and Jerozolimskie Avenue were widened and prolonged. The Łazienkowska Motorway linked the southern districts of left-bank Warsaw directly with Saska Kępa and Grochów; others arteries included the so-called Wisłostrada, joining Wilanów and Młociny, and Toruń Route, between Żerań, Ochota and Wola, to be completed in the year 2000.

Modern architecture, usually fulfilling residential or office functions, creates interesting enclaves in chaotic, at times semi-rural housing, or amidst the monotony of the barrack-like architecture of housing estates. Elegant and individual style is the distinguishing feature of the office buildings of the Arcon Industrial Service Corporation in Baletowa Street or Pomaton EMI in Osmańska Street, both from 1997–1998. In turn, among the numerous housing estates on the outskirts of the town, the one in Akacjowa Street (built in 1995–1997) displays an attractive combination of the employed construction materials. In Żoliborz, the housing estate in Hozjusz Street (1994–1997) refers to the functionalism of the 1930s. Several striking buildings were erected in 1996–1997 in such districts as Służewiec (the University Business Centre) and Wola, neglected from an architectural point of view. In the latter district, an office building recognised by the residents of the capital as a "Warsaw Favourite" was built in 1996–1997 in Kasprzak Street.

Królikarnia Palace, erected 1782–1786, project by Domenico Merlini

Monument of the Construction of Brzeska Highway, unveiled in Grochowska Street in 1825, bas- reliefs by Paweł Maliński

Situated on the right bank of the Vistula, Praga was associated closely with the fate of left-bank Warsaw. Administratively divided into North and South, its present-day area totals more than 230 square kilometres. Road and railway bridges connect it rather effectively with the left bank, although the absence of sufficient bridge communication remains discernible, especially in the southern part of the capital.

Praga owes the considerable preservation of its historical spatial configuration and old housing, mainly from the end of the nineteenth century and the beginning of the twentieth century, to relatively slight wartime damage.

The district originated from a series of mediaeval villages: Bródno, Kamion and Gocław, which arose in the tenth and eleventh centuries, as well as to the slightly later Grochów, Kawęczyn, Miedzeszyn, Zastów and Zerzeń in the south and Praga, Żerań, Golędzinów and Targowe Wielkie in the north. The name of the district comes from the village of Praga, situated during the fifteenth century in the region of present-day Targowa Street.

During the seventeenth and eighteenth century, similarly to Warsaw, the basic settlement units in Praga were the jurisdictions (*jurydyki*). The 1640s witnessed the foundation of Skaryszew, Praga Biskupia (Bishop's Praga), and Praga Książęca (Ducal), or Magnacka (Magnate Praga), among which Praga Biskupia stood out due to the erection of one of the earliest large churches on the right bank (1630s); this was the Bernardine church, pulled down during the nineteenth century. The favourably progressing Prague jurisdictions were seriously damaged during the battle for Warsaw, waged with the Swedes in 1656.

In the second half of the eighteenth century, the urbanised area and nearby villages were purchased by Stanisław Augustus. In 1764, the King bought Targówek, which he ordered to be divided into plots; he also arranged for a Royal Zoological Garden to be set up on the vast area to the north of the village. In the same year, Stanisław Augustus became the owner of part of Golędzinów, and founded the Golędzinów Królewski (Royal Golędzinów) jurisdiction. More than a decade later, in 1780, he expanded his property in Praga by purchasing Kamion and Skaryszew, property of the Płock chapter, as well as the villages of Grochów, Kawęczyn and Gocław, which he subsequently presented to his nephew, Stanisław Poniatowski, who in today's Grochowska, Grenadierów and Podskarbińska streets created the jurisdiction of Kamion. In this manner, during the reign of Stanisław Augustus there were five jurisdictions on the right bank of the Vistula: Kamion and Skaryszew, followed by Praga Książęca, Praga Biskupia and Golędzinów Królewski (from the south to the north). In 1792, Praga had a population of 7 200, the majority being engaged in trade and the crafts. As in the case of Warsaw, Praga (Biskupia, Magnacka, Golędzinów and Kamion) was surrounded by the bulwarks erected by Marshal Lubomirski in 1770; in 1791–1794, this area, together with Skaryszew, became part of Warsaw.

During the Kościuszko Insurrection, a bloody battle waged on 4 September 1794 in the defence of Praga ended with the capture of the right

bank by the Russian armies, the cruel massacre of the local population and a conflagration destroying almost all the houses. Successive losses were incurred in Praga in 1806–1811, when many of the houses were demolished to make way for fortifications built by the Napoleonic army.

A brief period of prosperity occurred at the time of the Kingdom of Poland (1815–1830), when the villages of Targówek and Nowe Bródno changed into suburban settlements, and the old wooden buildings in the streets of Praga became accompanied increasingly frequently by brick houses. Hostilities connected with the November Uprising of 1830–1831 led to consecutive damage.

For a long time, Praga remained a neglected district; a regulation of the extensive area between the Vistula and Targowa Street was inaugurated after 1860, in connection with the construction of the Kierbedź Bridge and the opening of the St. Petersburg and Terespol railway lines. In accordance with the regulation plan accepted in 1864, the centre of this urban layout was located in a square (later: Weteranów /Veterans'/) along the axis of a street leading from the bridge. Present-day Zygmuntowska, Floriańska, Sierakowski, and Łukasiński streets radiated from the square, with Floriańska and Łukasiński streets leading to the newly delineated Jagiellońska Street.

The construction of the Kierbedź Bridge and, at the beginning of the twentieth century, of the Poniatowski Bridge, together with the location of railway stations resulted in the extremely rapid development of right-bank Warsaw. The spatial configuration of Praga was defined by railway line tracks, whose framework embraced small districts of this part of town. Nowa Praga was situated between the tracks of the circular railway and the St. Petersburg line. The horseshoe pattern of the tracks of the St. Petersburg and Terespol lines included a part of Targówek known as Szmulowizna, together with its central streets: Kawęczyńska, Ząbkowska and Radzymińska. Ząbkowska Street became linked with the newly marked Brzeska Street. The district of Kamionek stretched between the Terespol railway line and Grochowska Street; its spatial base was the southern part of Targowa Street, as well as Grochowska and Lubelska streets. Targowa Street was connected with Lubelska Street by the recently marked Skaryszewska Street. A new network of streets emerged also to the north-east of Grochowska Street, while to the north of the circular railway line there appeared new settlements crossed by the tracks of the Vistula line – Pelcowizna, closer to the Vistula, and Bródno, on the other side of the tracks. In eastern Praga, immediately beyond the tracks of the circular line, there lay the remaining part of Targówek; Radzymińska Street became the base for a network of newly marked streets.

Over the panorama of Praga there towered two newly erected churches: the Russian Orthodox church of St. Mary Magdalene (1867–1869) and the church of St. Florian (1888–1901). Large industrial enterprises were built in Targówek and in Nowa Praga, Szmulowizna and Kamionek, the latter being incorporated into Warsaw in 1880. One of the largest cemeteries in Europe was established in Bródno in 1884, and the Skaryszew Park dates back to 1910–1915.

Russian Orthodox church of St. Mary Magdalene in the Praga district (Solidarności Avenue), built in 1867–1869 acc. to a design by Nikolai A. Sichev

House at the junction of Szeroka and Targowa streets in the Praga district, erected about 1910

House in Targowa Street in the Praga district, built in 1890–1900

Building of the Head Office of the Polish State Railway in Targowa Street in the Praga district, erected in 1928–1930 acc. to a project by Marian Lalewicz

Intensive growth of Praga took place during the inter-war period. The majority of the wooden buildings, still numerous prior to the first world war, was replaced by brick housing. New monumental state buildings included the seat of the Main Office of the State Railways in Targowa Street, and numerous factories and industrial enterprises – the E. Wedel Chocolate Factory; in 1927, the Zoological Garden was opened in Prague Park. Poniatowski Avenue (later Washington) was extended to Grochowska Street (about 1926). There appeared two roundabouts – one next to the Skaryszew Park, and the other at the intersection of Grochowska and Wiatraczna streets. The largest-range division of land into building plots was carried out in Saska Kępa and Grochowska Street as well as in smaller areas, in Targówek and Pelcowizna.

Particular attention is due to Saska Kępa, situated at some distance from the centre of Praga. Its fate always followed a slightly different course – according to chronicles, during the fourteenth century it was the property of burghers, and during the seventeenth century – of Dutch settlers (at that time, it was known as Kępa Holenderska). The present-day name comes from the period when Poland was ruled by Saxon kings from the Wettin dynasty; the royal court of Augustus III sought entertainment in Saska Kępa, which retained this character throughout the eighteenth century and the entire nineteenth century. In the inter-war period, this was one of the most luxurious districts of Warsaw, full of modern villas.

Residential house for workers of the State Railway in Targowa Street in the Praga district, built in 1925 acc. to a project by Henryk Julian Gay

The second world war caused the partial damage of Praga, although to a degree much slighter than in left-bank Warsaw. A considerable part of the Praga houses were rebuilt in 1945-1950; immediately after the war, the seats of central offices and the municipal authorities were located in this district. In the successive years, Praga became an area of intensive development – the first residential estate was Praga I, built in 1948–1952. The area of Praga increased in each consecutive decade, and in the 1980s the district reached as far as Tarchomin, Białołęka, Henryków and Choszczówka. Żerań became the largest Warsaw industrial district.

Fortunately, the new estates and industry were situated predominantly in areas which became part of Warsaw in 1951, in this way preserving the characteristic network of streets and a considerable fragment of the former centre of Praga. Extant relics of Warsaw town folklore are symbolised by the Różycki Bazaar. Strolling along the streets of Praga and gazing into the courtyards of the old houses, we may still capture the atmosphere of Old Warsaw. The landscape of old Praga continues to be dominated by the towers of the church of St. Florian and the dome of the Russian Orthodox church of St. Mary Magdalene, while the very nature of the houses is determined by neo-historical, Art Nouveau or modernistic architecture.

The post-1989 investment tide has not bypassed Praga, although it is not as intensive as on the left bank. Distinct accents of contemporaneity include numerous trade-service centres or residential housing, such as the house in Piotr Skarga Street in Targówek (1995–1997).

Church of St. Michael and Florian in the Praga district, erected in 1887–1901 acc. to a project by Józef Pius Dziekoński; reconstructed in 1947–1972

→

Graphic design
KRZYSZTOF FINDZIŃSKI

Translation
ALEKSANDRA RODZIŃSKA-CHOJNOWSKA

Verification
PETER MARTYN

ISBN 83-213-4161-6

Arkady Publishing House Ltd., 00-344 Warsaw, 28 Dobra Street
tel. (48 22) 635-83-44, fax (48 22) 827-41-94
e-mail: arkady@arkady. com.pl
1st edition, 2000. Symbol 3254/R
Typesetting and layout: Agencja MASTER, Łódź
Printed by Olsztyńskie Zakłady Graficzne S.A.